THE AVOII ATTACHMENT RECOVERY

BIBLE

From Fear to Secure Attachment

Unlock Emotional Intimacy, Decode Your Heart's Secrets, Unveil Deactivation and Forge Lasting Bonds

4 BOOKS IN 1

By Esther Collins

Extra Bonus

Inside the book

Scroll to the end and scan the QR Code

Table of Contents

Introduction

Welcome and How to Navigate This Workbook

Welcome to the "Avoidant Attachment Recovery Workbook," a guide designed to lead you through the complexities of attachment theory and into a place of personal growth and stronger relationships. Whether you've stumbled upon this workbook out of curiosity or you're here by recommendation, know that you've taken a brave first step towards understanding and transforming your attachment style.

This workbook is structured to gradually build your knowledge and self-awareness, layer by layer. It is both a map and a companion on your journey towards emotional well-being. Here's how to make the most of it:

1. Take Your Time: There's no rush. The path to understanding your attachment style is not a race. Read at a pace that feels comfortable, and give yourself space to reflect on each new piece of information.

2. Reflective Exercises: Throughout the book, you'll encounter exercises designed to prompt introspection. These are opportunities to pause and engage deeply with the content, applying it to your own life. Keep a notebook or journal handy to record your thoughts and discoveries.

3. Practical Tools: Each chapter includes strategies and tools that you can implement in your daily life. Treat these as experiments in living differently, and observe what changes they bring about in your thoughts, feelings, and relationships.

4. Openness to Change: Approach the workbook with a willingness to encounter new ideas about yourself. Be ready to question old patterns and consider new ways of relating to others.

5. Seek Support if Needed: The journey can stir up strong emotions. If at any point you feel overwhelmed, consider seeking support from a therapist or a support group.

6. Revisit as Needed: Your relationship with this workbook doesn't end upon reaching the last page. As you grow and change, different sections will take on new meanings. Revisit them as often as you like.

7. Honor Your Progress: Acknowledge each step you take, no matter how small. Every bit of insight you gain is a piece of the puzzle that is your path to secure attachment.

As you move through the workbook, remember that it is a tool among many. It can be used in conjunction with therapy or as part of a self-directed journey. It is here to provide clarity, guidance, and hope. May you find within its pages the keys to unlock a more connected, fulfilling way of living and loving.

Now, let's turn the page and begin with an exploration of the science of attachment, as we set out on this transformative voyage together.

The Science of Attachment: A Modern Understanding

Attachment theory, first articulated by John Bowlby and Mary Ainsworth in the mid-20th century, has evolved significantly over the decades. Initially developed to understand the nature of the emotional bond between infants and their primary caregivers, it has since been expanded to explore how these early attachment styles impact adult relationships. This chapter will delve into the foundational concepts of attachment theory, explore its evolution, and discuss its relevance in contemporary psychology.

The Roots of Attachment Theory

John Bowlby: The Pioneer

John Bowlby, the father of attachment theory, posited that the bonds formed between a child and their primary caregiver have profound implications that extend well into adulthood. He believed that these early experiences influence our expectations and behaviors in relationships throughout life.

Mary Ainsworth: The Strange Situation

Mary Ainsworth, a colleague of Bowlby, further refined the theory with her groundbreaking research, known as the Strange Situation. This study categorized attachment into three primary styles based on children's behavior when separated and reunited with their caregiver: secure, anxious-ambivalent, and avoidant.

Since its inception, attachment theory has expanded beyond the confines of mother-child interactions. Researchers have applied the theory to adult relationships, examining how these foundational attachment styles influence romantic partnerships, friendships, and even workplace dynamics.

Adult Attachment Models

The application of attachment theory to adults led to the development of two key models:

- The Bartholomew Model categorizes adult attachment into four types: secure, dismissive-avoidant, fearful-avoidant, and preoccupied.
- The Dynamic-Maturational Model (DMM) of attachment and adaptation stresses that attachment is not static and can change with new relational experiences and personal growth.

Attachment Styles Explained

Secure Attachment

Characterized by a positive view of self and others, secure attachment is formed in an environment where caregivers are consistently responsive and supportive. Adults with secure attachment tend to have healthy, stable relationships.

Avoidant Attachment (Dismissive and Fearful)

Avoidant attachment develops when caregivers are emotionally distant or unresponsive. Adults with dismissive-avoidant attachment often value independence to the extreme, avoiding closeness, while those with fearful-avoidant attachment desire closeness but fear being hurt.

Anxious Attachment

Originating from inconsistent caregiving, this style is marked by a negative self-view and a positive view of others. Adults with anxious attachment crave closeness but are plagued by fear of rejection.

Contemporary Research and Implications

Recent studies in neuroscience have illuminated how attachment styles are represented in the brain, affecting our emotional regulation and relationships. Neuroimaging shows that securely attached individuals have more developed neural networks for processing emotions, which contribute to their resilience in relationships.

Attachment in Therapy

Understanding one's attachment style is crucial in psychotherapy. Therapists often use attachment theory to help clients understand their relationship patterns and develop strategies for forming secure attachments.

Cultural Variations

It's important to note that attachment theories are influenced by cultural contexts. What constitutes secure attachment behaviors can vary widely across different societies, highlighting the need for a culturally sensitive approach to applying attachment theory.

Why Attachment Matters Today

The modern understanding of attachment theory offers vital insights into our interpersonal relationships and personal development. By understanding attachment styles, individuals can work towards healing insecure patterns and fostering more fulfilling, emotionally healthy relationships.

As we continue through this workbook, we will explore how you can identify your attachment style and use this knowledge to enhance your relationships and emotional well-being. Let this chapter serve as a foundational stone upon which we will build more specific strategies for growth and change.

Part I

Discovering the Roots

of

Avoidant Attachment

Chapter 1

The Attachment Spectrum

Attachment theory offers a lens through which we can view our relationships and understand our patterns of emotional interaction. This chapter explores the spectrum of attachment styles, beginning with the most functional and healthy— secure attachment.

Secure Attachment: The Ideal Benchmark

Secure attachment is considered the healthiest form of attachment and serves as the benchmark for emotional and relational stability. It originates from a caregiving environment where primary needs are met consistently and emotional communication is open and reciprocal. This foundational experience fosters a sense of safety and trust in relationships that influences behavior from childhood through adulthood.

Characteristics of Secure Attachment

- Self-Assurance: Securely attached individuals generally have a positive view of themselves and their self-worth. They feel capable and independent yet are comfortable seeking support when needed.
- Healthy Relationships: They tend to have stable and deep relationships characterized by mutual respect, empathy, and intimacy. Their relationships are typically free from the dramas that plague more insecure styles.

- Emotional Regulation: One of the hallmarks of secure attachment is the ability to manage emotions effectively. These individuals can handle stress and setbacks with resilience, maintaining emotional balance.
- Effective Communication: Open and honest communication is a strength of securely attached individuals. They are able to express their needs and feelings clearly and are also receptive to the feelings and needs of others.

Development of Secure Attachment

Secure attachment develops in an environment where caregivers are:

- Responsive: Caregivers meet the child's needs consistently and appropriately, providing comfort and attention.
- Attuned: They are finely tuned to the child's emotional states and respond to their cues effectively.
- Supportive: They encourage exploration and independence, providing a safe base from which the child can explore the world.

Impact on Adult Relationships

The influence of secure attachment extends far beyond childhood, shaping adult relationships in profound ways:

- Trust: Securely attached adults trust their partners and are trustworthy in return. This trust is foundational for building long-term committed relationships.
- Balance: They balance closeness with independence, valuing both intimacy and personal freedom.
- Conflict Resolution: These individuals handle conflicts constructively, without resorting to destructive behaviors. They can negotiate and compromise, seeking solutions that respect both partners' needs.

Why Secure Attachment Serves as a Benchmark

Secure attachment is considered the ideal because it provides the tools necessary for healthy relational and personal functioning. These tools include empathy, resilience, effective communication skills, and emotional intelligence. People with secure attachment are generally happier and more satisfied in their relationships and personal pursuits.

Striving for Security

Understanding secure attachment not only provides a goal for personal development but also offers a template for parenting. For those who did not develop secure attachments in childhood, the good news is that attachment styles are not set in stone. Through therapy, personal effort, and healthy relationships, it is possible to develop a more secure attachment style.

In the following sections, we will explore other attachment styles on the spectrum, offering insights into how they form and how one might journey toward security. As we delve deeper into the dismissive-avoidant, anxious-preoccupied, and fearful-avoidant styles, remember that the goal of this workbook is not just to understand where you might currently be on the attachment spectrum, but to guide you towards the secure attachment that offers the best foundation for fulfilling relationships and a contented life.

Dismissive-Avoidant: The Fortress of Solitude

The dismissive-avoidant attachment style is characterized by a profound need to remain independent and self-sufficient, often at the expense of interpersonal closeness and intimacy. This section explores the hallmarks of dismissive-avoidant attachment, its origins, and its effects on relationships.

Characteristics of Dismissive-Avoidant Attachment

Individuals with a dismissive-avoidant attachment style typically exhibit a strong preference for emotional distance from others. They value their autonomy highly and can often appear aloof or detached in relationships. Key characteristics include:

- Self-reliance: Dismissive-avoidant individuals pride themselves on their independence and ability to handle life's challenges without assistance.
- Emotional detachment: They tend to distance themselves emotionally from others, often minimizing the importance of relationships.
- Discomfort with intimacy: Closeness in relationships can be unsettling for them, leading to behaviors that maintain their personal space and autonomy.
- View of relationships as non-essential: They often see relationships as less important than personal goals and self-sufficiency.

Origins of Dismissive-Avoidant Attachment

Dismissive-avoidant attachment often develops in early childhood, where the emotional availability of caregivers was inconsistent or lacking. Key factors that contribute to the formation of this attachment style include:

- Emotionally distant caregiving: Caregivers may have been unresponsive to the child's emotional needs, often encouraging premature self-reliance.

- Valuing independence: Families that prize independence and discourage expressions of vulnerability or neediness can foster dismissive-avoidant behaviors in children.
- Negative reinforcement: Children who learn that seeking support leads to disappointment may stop seeking it altogether, reinforcing the notion that they must go it alone.

Impact on Relationships

The way dismissive-avoidant individuals approach relationships can lead to specific challenges:

- Difficulty forming deep connections: Their discomfort with emotional closeness can prevent the development of deep, meaningful relationships.
- Perceived aloofness: Partners may view their need for distance as indifference or a lack of interest.
- Avoidance of dependency: They often avoid situations that might put them in a position of dependency, preferring instead to remain in control and unattached.
- Conflict avoidance: Dismissive-avoidant individuals tend to withdraw from conflict or dismiss issues rather than engaging in emotional discussions.

Moving Toward Security

Despite the challenges, individuals with a dismissive-avoidant attachment style can move towards more secure attachment patterns. Strategies for this transformation include:

- Recognizing the value of relationships: Understanding and appreciating the benefits of close relationships can be a first step toward valuing interpersonal connections.
- Gradual engagement in emotional closeness: Slowly and intentionally engaging in activities that promote emotional intimacy can help ease the discomfort associated with closeness.
- Therapy and self-reflection: Professional help can be crucial in unpacking the roots of avoidant behaviors and developing healthier relationship skills.
- Mindfulness practices: These can enhance emotional awareness and regulation, helping individuals respond more openly to relational cues.

While the fortress of solitude might initially seem like a safe haven, over time, it can become a lonely place. Recognizing and addressing the underlying fears and beliefs that perpetuate dismissive-avoidant attachment can open the door to richer, more fulfilling interpersonal experiences. The journey toward secure attachment involves embracing vulnerability as a strength rather than a liability, paving the way for deeper and more satisfying connections.

Anxious-Preoccupied: The Tug of War

Anxious-preoccupied attachment is marked by a persistent concern about being unloved and a fear of abandonment. This attachment style is characterized by high emotional reactivity and sensitivity to relationship dynamics, often resulting in a tumultuous and insecure relational pattern. This section examines the defining traits, origins, and interpersonal effects of the anxious-preoccupied attachment style.

Characteristics of Anxious-Preoccupied Attachment

Individuals with an anxious-preoccupied attachment style display a continuous need for closeness and reassurance, which can overwhelm their partners and lead to cycles of conflict and reconciliation. Key traits include:

- High sensitivity to partners' actions and moods: They often read into small behaviors and overinterpret them as signs of rejection or disinterest.
- Seeking validation and approval: There is a compelling need to be liked and approved of, often going to great lengths to please others at the expense of their own well-being.
- Fear of abandonment: Even minor separations or changes in a partner's behavior can trigger intense fear and insecurity.
- Emotional volatility: Their relationships are often intense but unstable, marked by frequent ups and downs.

Origins of Anxious-Preoccupied Attachment

The development of an anxious-preoccupied attachment style can usually be traced back to childhood experiences where emotional responsiveness from caregivers was unpredictable. Factors influencing this attachment style include:

- Inconsistent caregiving: Caregivers alternated between warmth and availability and coldness or indifference, leading to confusion and insecurity about relational stability.
- Hyper-attunement to others' emotional states: Growing up in environments where they had to constantly gauge the emotional climate to predict and react to caregivers' responses.
- Modeling of anxious behaviors: Often, caregivers themselves displayed anxious attachment behaviors, serving as models for relationship dynamics.

Impact on Relationships

The anxious-preoccupied attachment style affects relationships in several profound ways:

- Clinginess and dependency: This attachment style often leads to dependency on relationship partners for emotional security and self-esteem.
- Conflict escalation: Small disagreements can quickly escalate into significant conflicts due to their heightened emotional responses and fears of loss.
- Sacrificing personal boundaries: In their quest for closeness, they often compromise their own needs and boundaries, which can lead to resentment and burnout.
- Reassurance-seeking behaviors: They frequently seek reassurance to quell their insecurities, which can strain relationships and sometimes lead to the very rejection they fear.

Moving Toward Security

Moving towards a more secure attachment style involves addressing the deep-seated insecurities and fears that drive the anxious-preoccupied behaviors. Effective strategies include:

- Developing self-awareness: Recognizing and understanding their own attachment patterns is a critical first step.
- Building self-esteem: Focusing on personal development and self-care can reduce their dependency on others for validation.
- Learning to regulate emotions: Emotional regulation skills can help manage their reactivity and reduce the intensity of emotional swings.
- Therapy and counseling: Professional help can provide strategies for dealing with past trauma and learning healthier ways of relating to others.

- Practicing effective communication: Learning to communicate needs and desires clearly and constructively without fear or aggression.

For individuals struggling with anxious-preoccupied attachment, the path to secure attachment involves understanding their worth independent of their relationships, improving emotional self-regulation, and fostering genuine intimacy based on mutual respect and understanding.

Fearful-Avoidant: The Paradoxical Labyrinth

Fearful-avoidant attachment, also known as disorganized attachment, encapsulates a complex interplay of avoidance and anxiety. Individuals with this style experience conflicting desires: they crave closeness and intimacy but simultaneously fear the vulnerability that comes with it. This chapter explores the intricate dynamics of fearful-avoidant attachment, its origins, characteristics, and the profound impact it can have on personal relationships.

Characteristics of Fearful-Avoidant Attachment

People with fearful-avoidant attachment are often caught in a cycle of pushing away and then pulling people close, reflecting their internal conflict and confusion about relational intimacy. Key characteristics include:

- Mixed signals: They can oscillate between intense closeness and sudden withdrawal, confusing partners and often destabilizing relationships.
- Fear of intimacy: Despite their deep longing for connection, they are scared of being too emotionally close to someone, fearing eventual hurt or rejection.
- High emotional sensitivity: They are usually very sensitive to signs of rejection or abandonment, often reacting strongly to such perceived threats.

- Distrust of others: Their experiences often lead them to view relationships as fundamentally unsafe and other people as unreliable.
- Self-protective: They engage in behaviors that are meant to protect themselves from emotional pain, which can include mistrust, suspicion, and withdrawal even in seemingly secure relationships.

Origins of Fearful-Avoidant Attachment

Fearful-avoidant attachment typically develops in an environment where the child felt unsafe or experienced great inconsistency in emotional support. Key factors contributing to this attachment style include:

- Traumatic experiences: Exposure to trauma, especially where caregivers were the source of fear or were frightening themselves.
- Unresolved fears: Caregivers might have been dealing with their own unresolved traumas or fears, incapable of providing consistent and safe emotional support.
- Neglect or abuse: Early experiences of neglect or abuse can profoundly affect one's ability to trust others and form healthy attachments.

Impact on Relationships

The impact of fearful-avoidant attachment on relationships is characterized by volatility and complexity:

- Relationship turbulence: Their relationships are often fraught with ups and downs due to their conflicting desires for intimacy and distance.
- Sabotaging connections: They may unconsciously sabotage relationships as they near intimacy, driven by fear of potential pain or betrayal.

- Struggle with trust: Building and maintaining trust is challenging, as their inherent distrust and fear can overshadow moments of genuine closeness.
- Emotional isolation: In an effort to protect themselves, individuals with this attachment style might isolate themselves emotionally, even in committed relationships.

Moving Toward Security

Transitioning towards a more secure attachment requires addressing both the fear of intimacy and the instinct to avoid it. Effective strategies include:

- Therapeutic interventions: Therapy can help address and heal from past traumas, providing a safer space to explore vulnerabilities and fears without judgment.
- Gradual exposure to intimacy: Slowly building up exposure to intimacy can help reduce fear over time, allowing them to experience closeness without overwhelming anxiety.
- Building trust incrementally: Trust is a crucial component that needs nurturing in small, consistent steps.
- Emotional regulation skills: Developing skills to manage and understand their emotions can decrease reactivity and help them communicate more effectively in relationships.

For those with fearful-avoidant attachment, understanding the source of their fears and actively working towards healing can open up new pathways to deeper, more satisfying relationships. The journey involves unraveling the complexities of their fears, slowly building trust in themselves and others, and ultimately finding a balance between their needs for intimacy and independence.

Attachment Styles Assessment Tool

A comprehensive scoring assessment to determine which attachment style an individual aligns with most closely involves developing a series of questions that reflect typical thoughts, behaviors, and reactions in various relational contexts. This tool should offer a professional level of self-analysis and insight into one's attachment model, helping individuals understand their patterns in relationships.

Objective

To help individuals identify their predominant attachment style (Secure, Anxious-Preoccupied, Dismissive-Avoidant, Fearful-Avoidant) based on their responses to various relational scenarios.

Instructions

For each question, choose the option that most closely describes how you typically respond in relationship situations. Each choice corresponds to one of the four attachment styles: Secure, Anxious, Dismissive-Avoidant, and Fearful-Avoidant
Each question below is linked to typical reactions from each attachment style. Respondents will choose the option that best describes their usual response in such situations.

After completing all questions, tally the points for each category. The highest score indicates your predominant attachment style. The results will provide insights into your behavioral patterns in relationships and suggest areas for potential growth or improvement.
This tool can be incredibly valuable for individuals looking to deepen their understanding of their attachment style and improve their relational health.

Question 1: When you experience a disagreement with your partner, how do you typically respond?

- A. I try to understand their perspective and resolve the issue collaboratively. **(Secure: +2 points)**
- B. I become anxious and need reassurance that the relationship is still secure. **(Anxious: +2 points)**
- C. I prefer to avoid the confrontation and might withdraw from the discussion. **(Avoidant: +2 points)**
- D. I fluctuate between wanting to resolve the issue and wanting to withdraw. **(Fearful-Avoidant: +2 points)**

Question 2: How do you feel when a relationship in your life becomes intensely intimate?

- A. I feel comfortable and happy with the deepening connection. **(Secure: +2 points)**
- B. I feel nervous and insecure, worried about the relationship's sustainability. **(Anxious: +2 points)**
- C. I feel suffocated and look for ways to regain some space. **(Avoidant: +2 points)**
- D. I have mixed feelings, desiring closeness but fearing it at the same time. **(Fearful-Avoidant: +2 points)**

Question 3: If your partner does not respond to a message quickly, what is your typical thought process?

- A. They're likely busy; they'll respond when they can. **(Secure: +2 points)**
- B. They might be losing interest in me. **(Anxious: +2 points)**
- C. I hardly notice; I'm not concerned about the frequency of communication. **(Avoidant: +2 points)**

- D. I worry initially but try to rationalize that they might just be busy. **(Fearful-Avoidant: +2 points)**

Question 4: How do you typically handle feelings of jealousy in a relationship?

- A. I discuss my feelings openly to understand and resolve them. **(Secure: +2 points)**
- B. I often feel overwhelmed and seek reassurance. **(Anxious: +2 points)**
- C. I ignore these feelings or deny their importance. **(Avoidant: +2 points)**
- D. I feel jealous but afraid to bring it up, leading to internal conflict. **(Fearful-Avoidant: +2 points)**

Question 5: When your partner asks for more closeness or time together, how do you react?

- A. I welcome it and look forward to spending more time together. **(Secure: +2 points)**
- B. I worry about why they need more and what I might be doing wrong. **(Anxious: +2 points)**
- C. I feel pressured and may need more personal space. **(Avoidant: +2 points)**
- D. I feel torn between wanting closeness and needing space. **(Fearful-Avoidant: +2 points)**

Question 6: Consider your reaction when a relationship ends:

- A. I am hurt but recover by reflecting and learning from the experience. **(Secure: +2 points)**
- B. I feel deeply wounded and struggle to move on. **(Anxious: +2 points)**
- C. I detach quickly and often feel relief. **(Avoidant: +2 points)**

- D. I experience a mix of relief and pain, and may dwell on the relationship for a long time. **(Fearful-Avoidant: +2 points)**

Question 7: How do you view your needs in comparison to those of your partner?

- A. I see our needs as equally important and strive for a balanced approach. **(Secure: +2 points)**
- B. I often prioritize their needs above my own to keep the peace. **(Anxious: +2 points)**
- C. I prioritize my independence and often dismiss their needs if they conflict with mine. **(Avoidant: +2 points)**
- D. I struggle to balance our needs, often oscillating between self-sacrifice and self-interest. **(Fearful-Avoidant: +2 points)**

Question 8: How do you typically respond to constructive criticism from your partner?

- A. I view it as an opportunity to grow and improve our relationship. **(Secure: +2 points)**
- B. I feel hurt and worry it may mean they are unhappy with me. **(Anxious: +2 points)**
- C. I often feel criticized and may respond defensively or dismissively. **(Avoidant: +2 points)**
- D. I feel threatened but recognize the potential for personal growth, leading to mixed emotions. **(Fearful-Avoidant: +2 points)**

Scoring Interpretation

Secure Attachment: 24-36 points from Secure responses

- **Characteristics**: Individuals with a secure attachment style are typically comfortable with both intimacy and independence. They handle conflicts constructively and are capable of empathetic communication, fostering a supportive and trusting environment in their relationships. Their stability and reliability make them excellent partners in both personal and professional settings.
- **Implications**: Those scoring in this range generally have healthy, balanced relationships. They are adept at navigating the give-and-take that is required for maintaining long-term connections and are likely to lead fulfilling relational lives.

Anxious Attachment: 24-36 points from Anxious responses

- **Characteristics**: Individuals with an anxious attachment style often exhibit a deep concern about their relationships. They may be overly sensitive to their partners' actions and reactions, interpreting them as signs of possible rejection or abandonment. This sensitivity can lead to intense emotional responses and behaviors driven by the fear of losing the relationship.
- **Implications**: People with high scores in anxious attachment may struggle with insecurity and may require constant reassurance and attention from their partners. Their relationships can be tumultuous, and they might benefit from learning strategies to manage their anxieties and develop a healthier self-image.

Avoidant Attachment: 24-36 points from Avoidant responses

- **Characteristics**: Those with an avoidant attachment style often show discomfort with closeness and a strong preference for independence over forming romantic bonds. They tend to minimize the importance of emotions, both their own and those of others, which can lead to a distancing or detached demeanor in relationships.
- **Implications**: Avoidant individuals may find it challenging to develop and maintain close personal relationships. They often benefit from exploring the root causes of their discomfort with intimacy and may need to work on opening up emotionally and allowing themselves to be vulnerable with trusted individuals.

Fearful-Avoidant Attachment: 24-36 points from Fearful-Avoidant responses

- **Characteristics**: Those with a fearful-avoidant attachment style experience mixed feelings about intimacy. While they desire closeness and connection, they also fear getting too close and being hurt. This conflict often results in inconsistent behavior, which can be confusing and unpredictable to their partners.
- **Implications**: Individuals scoring in the fearful-avoidant range are often caught in a cycle of pushing away and then pulling close to their partners. They may struggle with fluctuating emotions and behaviors that can hinder the stability of their relationships. Addressing these fears through therapy and personal reflection can help in achieving more stable and satisfying connections.

Dynamic Attachments: Fluidity Among Styles

Attachment theory traditionally categorizes individuals into distinct styles based on their predominant behaviors in relationships. However, it's essential to recognize that attachment is not static. People may exhibit characteristics of different attachment styles at various points in their lives or even in different relationships. This section explores the concept of dynamic attachments, emphasizing the fluidity and adaptability of attachment styles.

The Concept of Attachment Fluidity

Attachment fluidity refers to the idea that individuals can move across the attachment spectrum depending on life circumstances, personal growth, relationships, and therapy. This flexibility suggests that while our early experiences influence our attachment tendencies, we are not bound by them. Key insights into the fluidity among attachment styles include:

- Contextual Influences: People may display different attachment behaviors based on the context or environment. For example, someone might exhibit secure attachment traits in a trusting relationship but show anxious tendencies in a less reliable one.
- Life Transitions: Major life events such as marriage, parenthood, significant loss, or trauma can shift one's attachment style either temporarily or permanently.
- Relationship Dynamics: Interactions with significant others who have different attachment styles can influence and modify one's attachment behavior. For instance, a partnership with a secure individual may encourage a more secure attachment style in an anxious or avoidant partner.

Growth and Change in Attachment

Understanding that attachment styles can change offers hope and empowerment. It underscores the potential for growth and the possibility of developing more secure attachment patterns through conscious effort and therapeutic interventions. Ways to foster this growth include:

- Self-Awareness: Becoming aware of one's attachment style and its manifestations in relationships is the first step towards change.
- Relational Experiences: Positive and supportive relationships can serve as new models of attachment, teaching individuals healthier ways to relate and bond.

Enhancing Attachment Security

Strategies for moving towards a more secure attachment style focus on building the capacities that characterize secure attachments:

- Emotional Communication: Learning to express emotions clearly and sensitively can help enhance connection and intimacy.
- Consistent Responsiveness: Being consistently responsive and sensitive to the needs of others helps build trust and security in relationships.
- Reflection and Mindfulness: Reflective practices like mindfulness can increase emotional regulation and awareness, helping individuals respond more adaptively in relationships.

The dynamic nature of attachment teaches us that change is possible. Our attachment style is not a life sentence; rather, it is a starting point from which we can move towards greater security and healthier relationships. By understanding the fluid nature of attachment, individuals are better equipped to navigate the complexities of their relationships and foster enduring bonds built on trust, empathy, and mutual respect. This recognition of attachment's fluidity encourages a more compassionate and proactive approach to personal development and relational well-being.

Embracing the Possibility of Change

Understanding the fluidity of attachment styles is empowering, offering a hopeful perspective for those who wish to enhance their interpersonal relationships and overall emotional health. This section focuses on the importance of embracing change, exploring the ways in which individuals can actively work towards developing a more secure attachment style, regardless of their past experiences or current tendencies.

The Power of Neuroplasticity

At the heart of the possibility for change in attachment styles is the concept of neuroplasticity—the brain's ability to reorganize itself by forming new neural connections throughout life. This adaptability means that with intentional effort and the right strategies, individuals can reshape their attachment behaviors and reactions.

- Understanding Triggers: Recognizing and understanding what triggers insecure attachment behaviors is crucial. Awareness allows for the anticipation of reactions and the strategic planning of healthier responses.
- Cognitive Restructuring: By challenging and reframing negative thoughts about oneself and relationships, individuals can begin to alter their attachment

patterns. This involves replacing fears and insecurities with affirmations and evidence-based beliefs about self-worth and relational safety.

Therapeutic Interventions

Therapy offers a structured and supportive environment in which to explore one's attachment history and work through the barriers to secure attachment.

- Attachment-Based Therapy: This type of therapy focuses specifically on strengthening the security of attachments in adult relationships, addressing unresolved issues from one's childhood.
- Cognitive-Behavioral Therapy (CBT): CBT helps in identifying and changing negative thinking patterns and behaviors that result from insecure attachment styles.
- Dialectical Behavior Therapy (DBT): Particularly effective for those with fearful-avoidant attachment, DBT emphasizes the development of skills like mindfulness, emotional regulation, distress tolerance, and interpersonal effectiveness.

Building Secure Relationships

Creating and maintaining secure relationships also plays a vital role in the journey towards change. These relationships act as new models, demonstrating the principles of trust, mutual respect, and affection.

- Choosing Healthy Partnerships: Engaging with partners who exhibit secure attachment traits can foster similar behaviors in oneself.
- Open Communication: Developing a habit of open and honest communication in relationships can prevent misunderstandings and build trust.

- Vulnerability: Practicing vulnerability in safe environments can strengthen connections and reduce fears related to intimacy.

Personal Development and Support Networks

Change is not only about altering how one interacts in romantic relationships but also involves personal development and the support of a community.

- Self-care and Personal Growth: Engaging in activities that foster self-esteem and independence can reduce the anxieties associated with attachment insecurities.
- Support Groups: Participating in groups where members share similar struggles can provide emotional support and valuable insights, reinforcing the not-alone feeling.
- Continuous Learning: Education about attachment through books, workshops, and seminars can empower individuals with knowledge, which is a powerful tool for change.

Embracing Change as a Lifelong Journey

Change in attachment styles is not typically a quick fix but a lifelong journey. It requires persistence, courage, and the willingness to confront and heal from past wounds. By embracing the possibility of change, individuals open themselves up to the prospect of richer, more fulfilling relationships and a better understanding of themselves and others.

This commitment to growth not only enhances personal well-being but also contributes to healthier communities and societies, where empathy, understanding, and emotional connection prevail. As we move forward in this workbook, let each step taken be a step toward greater security and relational joy.

Chapter 1 Summary

This section delves into the attachment spectrum, positioning secure attachment as the optimal model for relational and emotional health. Secure attachment is characterized by traits such as self-assurance, emotional regulation, effective communication, and the capacity to maintain deep, stable relationships.

These traits stem from a caregiving environment that is responsive, emotionally attuned, and supportive, fostering a profound sense of safety and trust that extends into adult relationships.

Secure attachment affects how individuals handle trust, balance intimacy with independence, and manage conflict, making it an ideal because of its association with resilience, empathy, emotional intelligence, and general satisfaction in relationships. It is presented as a benchmark for readers to strive toward, emphasizing that attachment styles are adaptable and can evolve through therapeutic interventions, personal efforts, and healthy relationships.

The discussion also introduces other attachment styles that will be explored in greater depth later, including dismissive-avoidant, anxious-preoccupied, and fearful-avoidant. Each style is briefly described to prepare the reader for a deeper understanding of how these less secure attachments influence interpersonal dynamics and personal growth.

This foundational knowledge equips readers to navigate and potentially shift their own attachment styles towards more secure patterns, fostering healthier and more fulfilling relationships.

MY NOTES

Chapter 2

Roots and Routes

Tracing the Origins of Avoidant Attachment

Understanding the roots of avoidant attachment is crucial for anyone looking to reshape their relational patterns and build deeper, more meaningful connections. This chapter delves into the developmental origins of avoidant attachment, exploring how early experiences shape this attachment style and how it manifests throughout an individual's life.

The Developmental Context of Avoidant Attachment

Avoidant attachment typically develops in children who experience their caregivers as emotionally unavailable or unresponsive to their needs. These caregivers may have been present physically but often ignored or discouraged the expression of emotions, pushing the child toward premature self-sufficiency.

- Emotional Distance from Caregivers: Caregivers of avoidant children might not have rejected them outright, but often they did not respond to the child's cries for help or signals of emotional distress. This lack of response teaches the child to suppress their emotional needs.
- Valuing Independence Over Intimacy: In many cases, the caregivers of avoidantly attached children promote independence and self-reliance at an

age when emotional bonding and security are crucial. The subtle message communicated is that needing others is weak or undesirable.

- Lack of Physical Affection: Avoidant attachment can also stem from a lack of physical closeness and touch. Children whose emotional and physical needs for comfort are routinely dismissed or ignored learn to stop seeking comfort from others.

Psychological Underpinnings

The psychological landscape of someone with avoidant attachment is complex, often characterized by a strong sense of self-sufficiency paired with a deep-seated fear of dependence.

- Self-Image and Autonomy: Individuals with avoidant attachment often have a highly idealized self-image related to independence and self-reliance. They may view themselves as strong, not needing emotional support from others.
- Fear of Vulnerability: Underneath the surface, there is typically a profound fear of vulnerability. Being emotionally vulnerable is equated with being weak or exposed, which avoidant individuals strive to avoid.
- Suppression of Emotions: To maintain their self-image and avoid vulnerability, individuals with avoidant attachment frequently suppress their emotions. This suppression can lead to difficulties in recognizing and describing feelings, a condition known as alexithymia.

Manifestations in Adult Relationships

As children with avoidant attachment grow into adults, their early experiences profoundly influence how they form and maintain romantic relationships and friendships.

- Emotional Detachment: Adults with avoidant attachment often appear detached in their relationships. They may avoid deep emotional connections and prefer superficial or short-term relationships.
- Discomfort with Closeness: These individuals may feel uncomfortable with emotional closeness and intimacy. They might set strict boundaries in relationships to ensure that others do not get too close.
- Handling Conflict: Avoidantly attached adults tend to withdraw from conflict or ignore relationship issues. They prefer not to address emotional matters directly, which can frustrate partners seeking resolution and emotional depth.

Pathways to Change

Recognizing the origins of avoidant attachment can be the first step towards change. By understanding their early relational blueprints, individuals can begin to challenge their habitual patterns and explore new ways of connecting with others.

- Awareness and Acknowledgment: Acknowledging past experiences and their impacts is crucial. Awareness allows individuals to understand why they might be fearful of intimacy.
- Incremental Steps Toward Intimacy: Gradually increasing emotional disclosure and engagement can help individuals with avoidant attachment slowly build comfort with intimacy.

By tracing the roots of avoidant attachment and understanding its impact on relationships, individuals are better equipped to initiate and sustain the profound personal growth necessary for more secure and fulfilling connections.

Emotional Autarky: When Self-Reliance Becomes Isolation

In the spectrum of attachment styles, emotional autarky—the extreme self-reliance seen in those with avoidant attachment—can often lead to profound isolation. This section examines how a deep-seated emphasis on self-reliance, often rooted in early childhood experiences, can evolve into a counterproductive isolation that hinders personal growth and relationship satisfaction.

The Lure of Self-Reliance

For individuals with an avoidant attachment style, self-reliance is not just a personal trait but a survival strategy. Originating from early experiences where dependence on emotionally unavailable caregivers led to disappointment, these individuals learn to only rely on themselves.

- Independence as a Virtue: In many families that foster avoidant attachment, independence is highly valued, and needing others is often seen as a weakness or a burden. This can lead to a strong sense of pride in one's ability to cope alone, even in situations where seeking help would be beneficial.
- Fear of Dependency: The drive towards self-reliance is often fueled by a fear of dependency. There's a worry that relying on others could lead to being let down or hurt, so emotional walls are built to protect oneself.

The Shift to Isolation

What starts as a healthy desire for independence can become a limiting factor in one's life, as the line between self-reliance and isolation blurs.

- Social Withdrawal: Over time, the avoidance of emotional dependence can lead to withdrawal from social interactions and relationships. Individuals may decline opportunities for emotional intimacy, missing out on the support and pleasure that close relationships can offer.

- Suppression of Emotional Needs: Continually ignoring or suppressing one's emotional needs can lead to an inability to recognize or articulate these needs, even to oneself. This can result in feelings of emptiness or dissatisfaction with life, despite achievements in other areas.
- Relational Strain: In relationships, extreme self-reliance can be perceived as indifference or disinterest. Partners may feel unneeded and undervalued, leading to conflicts and disconnection.

Consequences of Emotional Isolation

The consequences of living in emotional autarky are significant, affecting various aspects of personal and social life.

- Emotional Distress: Constant suppression of emotional needs and desires can lead to increased stress, anxiety, and in some cases, depression. These individuals might struggle to understand the source of their distress, given their outward success in managing life independently.
- Relationship Dysfunction: The lack of emotional depth can prevent the formation of fulfilling relationships. Even in long-term relationships, partners may feel a persistent emotional distance that is difficult to bridge.
- Stunted Personal Growth: Without the challenge and support found in close relationships, personal growth can be stunted. Opportunities for self-improvement through feedback and reflection that come from deep interpersonal interactions are limited.

Navigating Towards Connection

Moving from isolation to connection involves recognizing the value of relationships and the strength in vulnerability.

- Reevaluating Self-Reliance: It begins with reevaluating the concept of self-reliance, understanding that true independence includes the ability to choose when to be dependent on others.
- Learning to Trust: Gradually allowing oneself to trust others can be practiced through small, incremental steps within safe and supportive relationships.
- Therapeutic Interventions: Engaging in therapy can provide a safe space to explore the deep-seated roots of one's self-reliance, offering strategies to slowly build comfort with intimacy and dependency.

Embracing emotional connection and interdependence can lead to richer, more fulfilling experiences. This shift not only enhances one's relationships but also supports personal well-being and emotional resilience. Recognizing the limits of emotional autarky is the first step toward opening oneself up to the growth and connection that come from balanced interdependence.

The Impacts of Avoidance on Self and Society

Avoidant attachment, characterized by a marked tendency to steer clear of close emotional connections, not only influences the individual exhibiting these traits but also ripples out to affect society at large. This section explores how avoidant behaviors impact personal well-being and interpersonal relationships across broader social contexts.

Personal Implications of Avoidant Attachment

For individuals with avoidant attachment, the repercussions of their relational style are profound and multifaceted, influencing their emotional landscape, psychological health, and life choices.

- Emotional Disconnect: Avoidants often experience an emotional disconnect, both from themselves and others. This detachment can lead to a diminished capacity for emotional awareness and expression, impacting their ability to experience life fully and richly.
- Compromised Psychological Health: Chronic avoidance of emotional closeness can lead to increased stress, anxiety, and depression. Over time, the lack of deep, supportive relationships can exacerbate feelings of loneliness and isolation, contributing to poorer mental health outcomes.
- Relationship Challenges: In personal relationships, whether romantic, familial, or platonic, avoidants may struggle to form and maintain close bonds. Their partners often feel a lack of intimacy and emotional availability, which can lead to dissatisfaction and conflict within relationships.

Societal Implications of Avoidant Attachment

When scaled to a societal level, the patterns seen in avoidant attachment can significantly affect social structures and cultural norms.

- Workplace Dynamics: In professional environments, avoidant individuals may contribute to a culture where emotional detachment and independence are overly valued. This can affect team cohesion and interpersonal understanding, potentially stifling collaboration and empathy-driven leadership.
- Community Engagement: Avoidant behaviors can influence community dynamics. Individuals who are emotionally withdrawn are less likely to engage

in community activities or support systems, weakening the social fabric and reducing communal support networks.

- Generational Impact: Parental avoidant attachment can influence the next generation, perpetuating cycles of emotional distancing and reduced intimacy. This transgenerational transmission of attachment styles can have long-term implications for societal emotional health and relationship patterns.

Addressing the Impacts of Avoidance

Understanding the broad impacts of avoidant attachment styles is crucial for developing strategies to address these issues both at an individual and societal level.

- Therapeutic and Educational Interventions: Promoting awareness and understanding of attachment styles through therapy and education can empower individuals to explore and modify their relational patterns. Therapeutic interventions can help individuals develop healthier ways of relating to others, fostering emotional closeness and community engagement.
- Enhancing Emotional Intelligence: Programs designed to enhance emotional intelligence in schools, workplaces, and communities can counteract the effects of avoidant behaviors. By teaching skills related to emotional awareness, communication, and empathy, societies can cultivate deeper interpersonal connections and resilience.
- Policy and Support Systems: At a policy level, creating supportive environments that encourage healthy parent-child attachments and address mental health issues can help mitigate the effects of avoidant attachment. Policies that promote parental leave, mental health support, and relationship counseling can support healthier societal relational dynamics.

The journey from avoidance to engagement involves not only personal transformation but also a shift in societal attitudes toward attachment and emotional expression. By addressing the root causes and manifestations of avoidant attachment, both individuals and societies can work toward a more connected and emotionally healthy future.

Chapter 2 Summary

This section explores the origins and impact of avoidant attachment, which typically begins in childhood with emotionally unavailable caregivers. These caregivers may be physically present but often discourage emotional expression, pushing children towards premature self-sufficiency and independence. This development fosters a strong sense of self-reliance in individuals, coupled with a deep-seated fear of dependence and vulnerability. As adults, this often manifests as emotional detachment, discomfort with closeness, and a tendency to withdraw from conflict, leading to superficial or strained relationships.

The concept of "emotional autarky" is introduced, describing how extreme self-reliance can lead to social withdrawal and relational strain, where individuals may suppress their emotional needs and partners may feel undervalued. The broader societal impacts of avoidant behaviors include less cohesive and empathetic workplace environments, diminished community engagement, and generational cycles of emotional distancing.

To address and overcome the limitations of avoidant attachment, the text recommends acknowledging past experiences, gradually increasing emotional intimacy, and seeking therapy. These steps are aimed at reevaluating self-reliance, fostering trust, and embracing interdependence, thus enabling richer and more fulfilling personal and societal relationships.

MY NOTES

Your Insight Can Illuminate the Path for Others

If you've reached this point in the book, you've journeyed deeply into the complex realms of attachment, intimacy, and personal growth, particularly addressing the challenges of avoidant attachment. You've tackled unveiling independence, vulnerability, and perhaps started reshaping your understanding of intimacy and trust. Now, you're invited to share your unique experiences and insights by leaving an honest review on Amazon. Your feedback not only reflects your own journey but also serves as a guiding light for others navigating similar paths in their relationships.

Imagine the Impact of Your Words

Think of how a single insight from this book changed your perspective or offered a moment of clarity. Your review could be the catalyst for similar epiphanies in others. It could encourage someone to start their journey towards emotional equilibrium, to embrace the discomfort of growth, or to seek understanding in the roots of their relational patterns.

Engage in a Greater Dialogue

Your review helps to weave a tapestry of collective insight that can support, guide, and inspire an entire community of readers. Each shared experience, each story of struggle and triumph, enriches this ongoing dialogue. It's not just about reviewing a book; it's about adding your voice to a chorus of narratives that can uplift and empower.

Thank You for Making a Difference

Your thoughts and experiences are a gift to this community. Together, we can support one another in transforming the way we relate to ourselves and those around us. Please take a moment to leave your honest review on Amazon, and let's continue to build a world where every voice is heard and every heart is understood.

Thank you for your courage to share, your willingness to help others, and your commitment to your journey of growth and healing.

Your voice matters.

Click here or scan this QR code to leave your review on Amazon if you live in the US

https://www.amazon.com/review/create-review/?asin=B0D3B6PH7Y

Click here or scan this QR code to leave your review on Amazon if you live in the UK

https://www.amazon.co.uk/review/create-review/?asin=B0D3B6PH7Y

Click here or scan this QR code to leave your review on Amazon if you live in the Canada

https://www.amazon.ca/review/create-review/?asin=B0D3B6PH7Y

Click here or scan this QR code to leave your review on Amazon if you live in the Australia

https://www.amazon.com.au/review/create-review/?asin=B0D3B6PH7Y

Part II

Managing Intimacy and Emotional Barriers

Chapter 3

Unveiling the Mask of Independence

The Myth of 'Not Needing Anyone'

The allure of independence resonates deeply in a culture that prizes self-sufficiency and individualism. However, for individuals with avoidant attachment styles, what often appears as a strong sense of independence can be a defensive mask hiding deeper fears of intimacy and vulnerability. This chapter explores the myth of not needing anyone, dissecting how this belief originates, its implications on personal relationships, and strategies for revealing and healing the underlying vulnerabilities.

The Origins of the Independence Myth

For those with an avoidant attachment style, the myth of complete independence often stems from early experiences with caregivers who were emotionally unavailable or inconsistently responsive. These initial interactions teach children that relying on others is unsafe or unrewarding, leading them to adopt self-sufficiency as a protective mechanism.

- Early Conditioning: Avoidants learn early to take care of themselves, believing that showing vulnerability or a need for help is a weakness that will lead to rejection or disappointment.

- Praise for Self-Sufficiency: Often, these individuals were praised for being independent from a young age, reinforcing the idea that self-reliance is a virtue to be aspired to, even at the cost of emotional connection.

Psychological Underpinnings

The psychological landscape of someone who upholds the myth of not needing anyone is complex and often involves suppressed emotions and unmet needs.

- Fear of Intimacy: Beneath the surface, the drive for independence is fueled by a deep-seated fear of intimacy and the vulnerabilities it brings. Emotional closeness is perceived as a threat to their autonomy and control.
- Emotional Suppression: In maintaining their independence, avoidants often suppress their emotional needs. This suppression can lead to difficulties in recognizing and expressing emotions, affecting their interpersonal relationships and overall emotional health.
- Self-Identity Tied to Autonomy: Their self-esteem is closely tied to their ability to be independent. Admitting a need for others can feel like a personal failure.

Impact on Relationships

The belief in absolute independence has significant implications for personal relationships, affecting everything from casual friendships to romantic partnerships.

- Distance in Relationships: Individuals clinging to this myth maintain a safe emotional distance from others, often at the expense of deeper connections. They might avoid situations that require emotional openness or vulnerability.

- Relationship Sabotage: Their relationships are frequently sabotaged by their withdrawal and reluctance to share more profound emotional truths. Partners may feel left out or undervalued, leading to frustration and conflict.
- Perpetual Loneliness: Ironically, the quest for independence can lead to isolation. Despite a robust outer facade, avoidant individuals often experience loneliness and a sense of disconnect from others.

Challenging the Myth

Breaking down the myth of not needing anyone involves confronting fears, reevaluating beliefs about independence, and gradually allowing for vulnerability within safe relationships.

- Acknowledging Needs: The first step is for individuals to acknowledge their emotional needs and the fundamental human necessity for connection and support.
- Gradual Exposure to Vulnerability: Practicing vulnerability can begin in small, manageable steps within trusted relationships. Sharing small personal concerns or worries can slowly build one's comfort with being vulnerable.
- Cultivating Emotional Awareness: Techniques such as mindfulness can help individuals become more aware of their emotions and gradually comfortable with expressing them to others.

Unveiling the mask of independence is not about renouncing self-sufficiency but about enriching one's life with the strength that comes from interdependence. By challenging the myth of not needing anyone, individuals with avoidant attachment can discover the joys and supports of deeper, more meaningful relationships.

Recognizing and Understanding Deactivation Strategies

Individuals with an avoidant attachment style often employ specific behaviors or psychological mechanisms to deactivate or suppress their need for closeness when they feel their independence is threatened. These deactivation strategies serve as a self-protective measure to maintain distance from others, thereby reducing their vulnerability to emotional discomfort. This section explores various common deactivation strategies, their implications, and how recognizing these patterns can lead to healthier relational dynamics.

What are Deactivation Strategies?

Deactivation strategies are tactics used by individuals with avoidant attachment to distance themselves emotionally from partners, friends, or family members when they sense emotional demands are increasing. These strategies can be subconscious and typically manifest in ways that sabotage closeness or intimacy.

- Withdrawal During Conflict: Instead of engaging in conflict resolution, avoidants often withdraw, shutting down communication and physically distancing themselves from the situation.
- Minimizing the Importance of Relationships: They may downplay the importance of close relationships or their emotional needs, portraying themselves as someone who does not require emotional support.
- Focus on Partners' Flaws: By focusing on a partner's imperfections, avoidants can justify their emotional distance and reluctance to commit further in a relationship.
- Avoidance of Physical Closeness: This can include avoiding physical touch, sex, or other forms of physical intimacy that typically promote emotional connection.

Psychological Basis of Deactivation

Deactivation strategies are rooted in the early relational experiences of individuals with avoidant attachment. As children, they might have learned that showing vulnerability or a need for emotional support would not be met positively by caregivers. Thus, they develop these strategies to control their environment and minimize perceived threats to their autonomy.

- Fear of Dependency: Avoidants often equate emotional closeness with dependency, which they perceive as a threat to their autonomy and control.
- Protection from Rejection: By deactivating their need for closeness, they protect themselves from the potential pain and rejection they associate with intimate relationships.

Recognizing Deactivation Strategies

Understanding and recognizing one's own deactivation strategies is a critical step toward change. Individuals can begin to see how these patterns manifest in their relationships and the impact they have.

- Reflective Journaling: Keeping a journal to record instances where one might feel the urge to pull away can help identify patterns and triggers of deactivation strategies.
- Feedback from Trusted Others: Sometimes, close friends, family members, or partners can provide insights into behaviors that might not be self-evident.

Moving Beyond Deactivation

Once deactivation strategies are recognized, individuals can work on strategies to manage and eventually reduce their use, fostering healthier interactions and relationships.

- Developing Awareness: Being mindful of the moments when deactivation strategies are employed allows individuals to choose different responses.
- Building Emotional Tolerance: Gradually increasing one's tolerance for emotional closeness can be facilitated through exercises in therapy, such as controlled exposure to situations that trigger deactivation, followed by discussion and reflection.

By understanding and addressing their deactivation strategies, individuals with avoidant attachment can begin to dismantle the barriers they have built around their emotions, paving the way for more fulfilling and intimate relationships. This process is not only about reducing the use of these strategies but also about embracing vulnerability as a strength, rather than a liability.

The Solo Journey: Appreciating Autonomy Without Avoidance

While autonomy is an essential aspect of a healthy personality and an integral component of human growth, its value is often misconstrued by those with avoidant attachment as a necessity to isolate oneself from emotional connections. This section explores how individuals can appreciate and cultivate true autonomy without resorting to avoidance, thus allowing for a balanced life that includes both independence and healthy relationships.

Defining Healthy Autonomy

Healthy autonomy is the ability to self-govern, make choices independently, and manage life's responsibilities without undue influence from others, while still maintaining fulfilling relationships. It is characterized by a sense of self-confidence and personal integrity that is not at odds with closeness to others.

- Self-Determination: Individuals make their own choices and take responsibility for these decisions without feeling the need to detach from others.
- Interdependence: Recognizing that being autonomous does not preclude one from engaging in mutually supportive relationships where both parties benefit.

Misconceptions of Autonomy in Avoidant Attachment

For those with avoidant attachment, autonomy often becomes entangled with avoidance, where independence is used as a shield against vulnerability.

- Equating Isolation with Independence: Avoidants may mistake emotional or physical distancing for autonomy, thinking that real independence means going through life without relying on anyone else.
- Fear of Enmeshment: There is often a deep-seated fear that any form of dependency or closeness will lead to a loss of self, which reinforces avoidance behaviors.

Strategies for Appreciating Autonomy Without Avoidance

Learning to appreciate true autonomy involves understanding its role in one's life and how it can coexist with healthy relationships.

- Building Self-Awareness: Engaging in introspection can help individuals understand their motives for seeking solitude and distinguish between healthy self-reliance and avoidance.
- Setting Boundaries: Effective boundary setting can help manage how much one engages with others, ensuring interactions are comfortable and do not compromise one's sense of autonomy.

- Developing Emotional Intelligence: Enhancing one's ability to recognize, understand, and manage emotions can lead to more robust autonomy. It allows individuals to respond rather than react to situations, maintaining their independence while engaging emotionally with others.

Embracing Interdependence

A key component of appreciating autonomy without falling into avoidance is embracing the concept of interdependence—the recognition that human beings are interconnected and that relationships can enhance personal freedom rather than diminish it.

- Recognizing the Value of Relationships: Understanding that supportive relationships can bolster personal growth and do not necessarily threaten autonomy.
- Practicing Vulnerability: Gradually opening up to others can strengthen autonomy by proving that one can be emotionally exposed without losing independence.
- Balancing Solitude and Social Interaction: Learning to enjoy solitude without using it as a way to escape from relational challenges, and engaging with others without feeling overwhelmed or losing oneself.

As we conclude Chapter 3, the transition from understanding and embracing true autonomy leads us naturally into Chapter 4, where we explore how these principles play out within the dynamics of intimate relationships. In "The Relationship Arena," we will delve into how individuals with an avoidant attachment style navigate intimacy and attachment dynamics, specifically focusing on how they manage their fears and desires in close relationships. This exploration will offer insights into the complex interplay between seeking independence and craving intimacy, highlighting the challenges and opportunities that arise in the quest for balanced, healthy relationships.

Chapter 3 Summary

This section addresses the myth of not needing anyone, particularly relevant to individuals with avoidant attachment styles. Often rooted in early experiences with emotionally unavailable caregivers, this belief serves as a defense against fears of intimacy and vulnerability. The pursuit of independence becomes a mask for a complex layer of suppressed emotions and unmet needs, leading to significant relationship challenges. Individuals often maintain emotional distance, sabotaging deeper connections and leading to isolation despite appearing self-content.

The narrative examines the psychological underpinnings of this attachment style, including common deactivation strategies used to suppress closeness, such as withdrawing during conflict and minimizing relationship importance. Recognizing and addressing these behaviors are crucial for fostering healthier relational dynamics and increased emotional awareness.

Additionally, the text explores the concept of true autonomy, distinguishing it from mere avoidance. True autonomy involves managing one's life independently while still engaging in fulfilling relationships, a balance that avoids the pitfalls of emotional isolation. Strategies to appreciate autonomy without avoidance include developing emotional intelligence and setting personal boundaries.

By challenging the ingrained views on independence and encouraging a shift towards embracing interdependence, the section aims to guide those with avoidant attachment towards a more balanced life that incorporates both autonomy and meaningful relationships. This understanding sets the stage for deeper engagement with the dynamics of intimate relationships in subsequent discussions.

MY NOTES

Chapter 4

The Relationship Arena

Navigating Intimacy: Dismantling Fears

Navigating the complexities of intimacy is a profound challenge for individuals with avoidant attachment styles. Their instinctual pull towards independence often clashes with the deeper human need for close and secure relationships. This chapter delves into how those with avoidant attachment can begin to dismantle their fears around intimacy, fostering healthier and more fulfilling connections.

Understanding the Fear of Intimacy

For avoidant individuals, intimacy invokes a paradoxical reaction: while there's a natural human longing for closeness, there's also a deep-seated fear that intimacy will lead to loss of independence or result in rejection and pain. These fears are not just emotional but are often embedded deeply in their subconscious, making them particularly challenging to address.

- Roots of Fear: The fear of intimacy often stems from early experiences where emotional closeness was associated with disappointment, intrusion, or abandonment. For avoidants, becoming close to someone means opening up to potential hurt or betrayal.

- Protection Through Distance: Maintaining emotional distance is a protective mechanism. It's a way to ensure that they never get too dependent on someone else, thus safeguarding their autonomy and avoiding the perceived dangers of vulnerability.

Strategies for Dismantling Fears

Breaking down the barriers to intimacy requires conscious effort and deliberate strategies to confront and modify ingrained behaviors.

- Incremental Exposure: Gradually increasing the level of emotional disclosure can help make the process less daunting. This could start with sharing small personal details or feelings and progressively working up to more significant, more vulnerable disclosures.
- Cognitive Reappraisal: Re-evaluating beliefs about intimacy and relationships can alter perceptions. For example, reframing vulnerability as a strength rather than a weakness can help reduce the associated fear.
- Mindfulness and Presence: Practicing mindfulness helps manage anxiety and fear by focusing on the present moment rather than worrying about potential future pains or dwelling on past hurts.

Building Trust and Safety

A key component of navigating intimacy is creating an environment where both partners feel safe and trusted. This is particularly crucial for those with avoidant attachment, who may have heightened sensitivity to any signs of control or engulfment.

- Consistent Communication: Establishing regular and open communication helps build trust. It reassures the avoidant partner that their needs and boundaries are respected.

- Mutual Understanding: Both partners should strive to understand each other's attachment styles and triggers. This awareness allows for more empathetic interactions and supportive behaviors.
- Creating Boundaries: Clearly defined boundaries help avoidants feel safe in intimacy because they know they can still maintain their independence and personal space.

As avoidants begin to dismantle their fears and build safer, more trusting relationships, they can experience the profound benefits of intimacy without feeling threatened by it. This journey requires patience, understanding from partners, and often professional guidance, but the rewards—a deeper, more connected relationship—are well worth the effort. The next sections will further explore specific dynamics within relationships involving avoidant individuals, including how they interact with other attachment styles and manage common relationship challenges.

Attachment and Dating Dynamics: Seeking the 'Unseekable'

For individuals with avoidant attachment, navigating the dating world can often feel like seeking the unseekable—pursuing relationships while simultaneously fearing the closeness they entail. This section explores how avoidant attachment influences dating behaviors, the challenges this presents, and strategies for forming healthier, more satisfying romantic connections.

The Paradox of Dating with Avoidant Attachment

Dating for those with avoidant attachment is fraught with contradictions. They may desire the companionship and intimacy that relationships offer but feel compelled to maintain a distance that prevents true closeness. This paradox manifests in several distinct behaviors:

- Elusive Commitment: Avoidant individuals often struggle with commitment, fearing it as a loss of freedom or an invitation for future hurt. They might avoid making long-term plans or expressing future goals with partners.
- Sabotage: Subconsciously, avoidants might sabotage relationships that get too close for comfort. This could be through nitpicking, creating conflicts out of minor issues, or pulling away emotionally when the relationship deepens.
- Idealizing Unavailable Partners: There's a tendency to idealize partners who are emotionally or geographically unavailable. Such relationships feel safer because they naturally enforce the distance that avoidants find comforting.

Understanding the Dynamics

The dating dynamics of avoidant individuals are deeply influenced by their underlying fears and protective mechanisms. Understanding these dynamics can help in addressing them:

- Fear of Enmeshment: Avoidants often confuse intimacy with enmeshment, viewing close relationships as a potential trap that could engulf their identity and independence.
- Control Over Emotions: They tend to control or suppress their emotions to avoid feeling vulnerable. This can make their emotional responses in relationships seem cold or detached.
- Independence Versus Isolation: There is often a thin line between valuing independence and isolating oneself. Avoidants need to recognize when their pursuit of independence is actually a shield against emotional intimacy.

Strategies for Healthier Dating

Navigating the dating world more effectively as an avoidant requires conscious efforts to understand and moderate the instinctual drive for distance:

- Awareness and Acceptance: Acknowledging their avoidant tendencies is the first step. This awareness can help in consciously adjusting behaviors that undermine relationship success.
- Communication Skills: Developing better communication skills can help avoidants express their needs and fears more clearly, reducing misunderstandings and conflicts in relationships.
- Choosing the Right Partner: Engaging with partners who are understanding and patient but also capable of maintaining healthy boundaries can help manage avoidant behaviors. Partners who are secure in their attachment can provide a stable base from which avoidants can explore intimacy safely.
- Personal Development: Personal Development can be a valuable tool for understanding and working through the fears that fuel avoidant attachment. Personal development activities that build self-esteem and emotional intelligence can also reduce reliance on avoidance strategies.

For avoidant individuals, seeking the 'unseekable' in dating doesn't have to be an endless cycle of pursuit and retreat. By understanding their attachment dynamics and working actively to address them, they can move towards forming relationships that honor their need for independence while also embracing the warmth and closeness of intimacy. The goal is to find a balance where relationships are experienced as enhancing rather than threatening personal freedom. This delicate balance can lead to more fulfilling and enduring partnerships, transforming the way avoidants experience love and connection.

When Two Avoidants Meet: The Unspoken Dance

When two individuals with avoidant attachment styles enter a relationship, it can result in a complex and often perplexing dynamic. Both partners, accustomed to maintaining emotional distance and safeguarding their independence, engage in what can be described as an "unspoken dance" of push and pull. This section delves into the dynamics of such relationships, exploring the challenges they face and the pathways to a healthier connection.

The Dynamics of Dual Avoidance

The interaction between two avoidant partners is characterized by mutual respect for independence but also a significant emotional distance that can be difficult to bridge.

- Mutual Independence: Both individuals typically appreciate and respect the other's need for space and autonomy. This mutual understanding can be comforting but also reinforces their tendencies to keep emotional distance.
- Conflict Avoidance: Since both partners tend to withdraw in times of stress or conflict, issues may remain unresolved, simmering beneath the surface and potentially leading to a buildup of resentment over time.
- Emotional Disconnection: There's often a lack of deep emotional connection, as both partners may struggle to express vulnerability and true intimacy. The relationship can sometimes feel more like a companionship or partnership devoid of deeper emotional ties.

Challenges Faced

The pairing of two avoidants brings unique challenges that can complicate the relationship dynamic.

- Stagnation in Intimacy: The relationship may plateau at a certain level of closeness, with both partners feeling unsatisfied but unsure how to deepen the emotional connection without triggering their fears of closeness.
- Lack of Emotional Support: In times of personal difficulty, both partners might find it hard to turn to each other for support, each assuming that the other prefers to cope independently, which can lead to feelings of isolation within the relationship.
- Resistance to Change: Since both partners typically resist emotional change and vulnerability, making progress toward a more connected relationship can be particularly challenging.

Navigating a Healthier Path

Despite the difficulties, there are ways for two avoidants to cultivate a healthier and more emotionally connected relationship.

- Open Communication About Attachment: Recognizing and discussing their avoidant attachment styles can help both partners understand the root of their behaviors and how these might be affecting their relationship.
- Joint Efforts in Therapy: Attending couples therapy can provide a safe space to explore their fears about intimacy and learn strategies to gradually open up to each other.
- Setting Intimacy Goals: Together, they can set small, manageable goals for increasing intimacy. This could involve regular check-ins about their feelings, shared activities that foster closeness, or simply spending more quality time together.
- Developing Shared Interests: Building a relationship around common interests can provide a safe medium for connection, reducing the focus on emotional vulnerability while still fostering a bond.

When two avoidants meet, the relationship requires careful navigation and a willingness to confront deeply ingrained fears of intimacy. By understanding and gently challenging their attachment behaviors, partners can slowly transform their unspoken dance into a more harmonious and emotionally satisfying relationship. This journey may not be easy, but with mutual dedication to growth, it can lead to a profoundly rewarding connection that neither thought possible.

Unlock Love: 5 Secret Scripts to Open Up an Avoidant Partner

Navigating a relationship with an avoidant partner can be challenging due to their natural tendency to distance themselves emotionally when feeling overwhelmed or pressured. However, with the right communication strategies, you can encourage openness and foster a deeper connection. Here are five "secret scripts" designed to help you engage more effectively with your avoidant partner, promoting understanding and closeness without triggering their withdrawal.

Script 1: When You Need More Emotional Closeness

Situation: Your partner seems distant after a stressful week.

Script: "I've noticed you seem a bit distant lately, and I imagine you might be feeling overwhelmed. I'm here if you want to talk about it, or if you prefer some quiet time together, that's okay too. How can I support you right now?"

Script 2: Encouraging Openness During Conflict

Situation: Your partner withdraws during an argument.

Script: "I realize this conversation might be uncomfortable, but I really value your perspective. Can we share our thoughts openly so we can understand each other better? I'll start by saying I might not have all the answers, but I want to find a solution together."

Script 3: Addressing Relationship Needs

Situation: You feel your emotional needs are not being met.
Script: "I feel loved when we share our day-to-day experiences with each other. It makes me feel connected to you. Can we set aside time each night to do this? What would make it comfortable for you to share more about your day?"

Script 4: When You Want to Discuss the Future

Situation: Discussing future plans which make your partner uncomfortable.
Script: "I know talking about the future can sometimes feel a bit daunting, but I think it's important for us to have these discussions to ensure we're aligned on our path forward. How can we approach this conversation in a way that feels safe for you?"

Script 5: Reinforcing the Positive

Situation: Your partner has shared something personal.
Script: "Thank you for sharing that with me, I know it's not always easy. I really appreciate you opening up like this, and it means a lot to me. Let's keep this communication going; I'm here to listen whenever you're ready."

How to Use These Scripts

- <u>Adapt Based on Context</u>: Feel free to modify the wording of these scripts to match the specific context of your conversation and the unique nature of your relationship.
- <u>Be Patient</u>: Remember that change doesn't happen overnight. Each of these scripts is designed to gradually help your partner feel more comfortable opening up.
- <u>Monitor Their Responses</u>: Pay attention to how your partner responds to different approaches. What works one day might not work another, so be flexible and adjust your approach as needed.

By using these scripts thoughtfully, you can help your avoidant partner feel safer and more comfortable in expressing themselves, thereby deepening the emotional connection between you. This is a gentle process of building trust and reinforcing the security of your relationship.

Recognizing Deactivation Triggers

In relationships, especially those involving an avoidant attachment style, recognizing and understanding deactivation triggers is crucial. These triggers are specific situations or behaviors that prompt a person with avoidant tendencies to pull away or shut down emotionally, often as a protective measure against perceived threats to their autonomy or safety. Identifying these triggers can help both partners manage reactions and foster a healthier, more connected relationship.

Understanding Deactivation Triggers

Avoidant individuals often deactivate or distance themselves in response to scenarios that invoke feelings of vulnerability, closeness, or dependency. Common triggers include:

- Intense Emotional Demands: High emotional expectations or demands can be overwhelming, causing the avoidant person to withdraw to regain their sense of control.
- Talks of Future Commitment: Discussions about future plans, such as moving in together or marriage, can trigger fear of loss of independence.
- Perceived Criticism or Conflict: Even constructive feedback or minor conflicts might be perceived as criticism or an attack, leading to withdrawal.
- Overwhelming Physical Closeness: Continuous physical proximity without personal space can make an avoidant partner feel trapped, prompting them to seek distance.
- Repeated Questions About Feelings: Persistent inquiries into their emotional state or feelings about the relationship can lead to discomfort and disengagement.

Strategies for Identifying Deactivation Triggers

Identifying triggers effectively involves careful observation and communication:

1. Observation and Reflection: Monitor patterns of behavior and note when and in what contexts your partner tends to pull away. Reflect on the events just before their withdrawal to identify potential triggers.
2. Open, Non-Threatening Conversations: Engage in discussions about triggers in a calm setting. Ask open-ended questions that encourage your partner to explore and express their feelings without the fear of judgment.

3. Journaling or Recording Observations: Keeping a journal of instances that led to deactivation can be helpful. Writing down emotions, settings, and conversations can help pinpoint specific triggers over time.

Managing Deactivation Triggers

Once triggers are identified, managing them involves both partners working together to create a supportive environment that respects the avoidant partner's needs while also fostering intimacy:

- Developing Gradual Exposure: Gradually increase emotional or physical closeness to help the avoidant partner become more comfortable over time, without overwhelming them.
- Creating Safety in Communication: Ensure that communications around sensitive topics are done in a manner that feels safe for the avoidant partner, using reassuring language and giving them control over the pace of the conversation.
- Establishing Boundaries: Define and respect personal boundaries together. This might include agreeing on times when it's okay to require space or setting limits on how often certain topics are brought up.
- Reinforcing Positive Interactions: Focus on reinforcing positive interactions after discussing triggers. Engaging in a shared activity that both partners enjoy can reinforce the security of the relationship.

By recognizing and sensitively managing deactivation triggers, couples can better navigate the complexities of avoidant attachment, leading to a more understanding and fulfilling relationship. This approach enhances communication and intimacy, contributing to a stronger bond.

The Interplay Between Avoidant and Anxious Partners

The relationship dynamic between an avoidant and an anxious partner is one of the most challenging yet common pairings in attachment theory. This volatile combination often results in a cycle of pursuit and withdrawal, where the needs and behaviors of each partner can exacerbate the insecurities of the other. This section explores the nuances of this interplay, the challenges it presents, and strategies for creating a more stable and fulfilling relationship.

Characteristics of the Avoidant-Anxious Dynamic

In relationships where one partner is avoidant and the other is anxious, their attachment styles create a push-pull dynamic that can be emotionally draining for both parties:

- Pursuit-Withdrawal Cycle: The anxious partner's need for closeness and reassurance can trigger the avoidant's fear of loss of independence and intimacy, leading to withdrawal. This withdrawal then intensifies the anxious partner's fears, leading to increased attempts at closeness and thus perpetuating the cycle.
- Conflict Escalation: The anxious partner's tendency to demand more commitment and reassurance can clash with the avoidant's need for space, leading to frequent conflicts that can escalate due to their differing coping mechanisms.
- Misaligned Communication Styles: Avoidant partners tend to minimize problems and avoid emotional discussions, which frustrates anxious partners who seek verbal reassurance and explicit communication about the relationship.

Understanding the Root of Conflicts

Understanding why these interactions become so charged is key to managing them effectively:

- Triggering Insecurities: Each partner inadvertently triggers the deepest insecurities of the other: avoidants fear being controlled or losing their autonomy, while anxious individuals fear abandonment and not being loved enough.
- Misinterpretation of Behaviors: Anxious partners might interpret the avoidant's need for space as rejection or lack of love, while avoidants might see the anxious partner's need for closeness as clinginess or dependency.

Strategies for Navigating the Avoidant-Anxious Relationship

Despite the inherent challenges, there are strategies that can help both partners find more harmony and understanding in their relationship:

- Enhanced Communication: Both partners need to develop more effective communication strategies that respect their differences. This might include setting aside time to talk about their feelings and concerns without criticism or avoidance.
- Understanding Each Other's Attachment Styles: Education about each other's attachment styles can go a long way in fostering empathy and patience. Knowing why a partner reacts a certain way can help the other respond more appropriately and compassionately.
- Balancing Needs: It's crucial for the relationship that each partner learns to balance their own needs with those of their partner. For the avoidant, this means occasionally stepping into closeness even when it feels uncomfortable. For the anxious partner, this involves allowing space without feeling abandoned or insecure.

- Couples Therapy: Working with a therapist can help resolve some of the entrenched patterns of interaction and provide both partners with tools to better manage their reactions and responses in the relationship.

Transition to Deeper Connection

As we transition from understanding the dynamics between avoidant and anxious partners, we move into exploring how couples can bridge the gap from maintaining distance to cultivating deeper intimacy. In the upcoming chapter, we will delve into how embracing emotional presence, committing to changing the script of retreat, and engaging in dialogues of vulnerability can transform relationships. These strategies are crucial for couples seeking to break free from the cycles of pursuit and withdrawal, paving the way for a more connected and mutually satisfying partnership.

Chapter 4 Summary

Navigating intimacy is a significant challenge for individuals with avoidant attachment styles, whose desire for independence often clashes with their need for close, secure relationships. This issue stems from early experiences where emotional closeness led to negative outcomes, prompting these individuals to maintain emotional distance as a defense against vulnerability.

The chapter provides strategies for dismantling these fears, including incremental exposure to vulnerability, cognitive reappraisal of relationship beliefs, and mindfulness to manage anxiety, shifting the view of independence from solitary to interdependent.

The dynamics of dating for avoidants, who may subconsciously sabotage relationships to preserve distance, are also explored, along with strategies to foster healthier dating behaviors like acknowledging avoidant tendencies and enhancing communication skills.

For relationships involving two avoidants, the chapter describes their interactions as an "unspoken dance" of maintaining distance, potentially leading to emotional disconnection. Recommendations for creating healthier connections include open communication about attachment styles and setting intimacy goals, possibly through joint therapy.

Additionally, "secret scripts" and insights into recognizing and managing deactivation triggers are provided to engage more effectively with avoidant partners and improve relationship dynamics.

Overall, the chapter emphasizes the importance of patience, understanding, and professional guidance in navigating the complexities of avoidant attachment and fostering deeper, more fulfilling relationships.

MY NOTES

Chapter 5

From The Trenches of Distance to the Bridges of Intimacy

Embracing Emotional Presence

The journey from distance to intimacy in relationships is a transformation that requires both partners, especially those familiar with avoidant or anxious attachment styles, to embrace emotional presence. This shift involves more than just physical closeness; it encompasses a full engagement with each other's emotional experiences, fostering a deeper understanding and connection. This section explores what it means to embrace emotional presence and how it can bridge the gap between partners, leading to a richer, more intimate relationship.

Understanding Emotional Presence

Emotional presence is the act of being fully engaged in the emotional climate of a moment or conversation with a partner. It means listening not just to respond, but to understand, empathize, and connect deeply with the other's feelings.

- Active Listening: This involves giving undivided attention to the partner while they speak, acknowledging their feelings without immediately trying to fix issues or offer advice.

- Empathetic Engagement: Understanding and sharing the feelings of the partner, empathetic engagement helps in creating a supportive environment that encourages openness and vulnerability.
- Nonverbal Communication: Often, emotional presence is conveyed through nonverbal cues such as eye contact, facial expressions, body language, and physical touch, all of which can significantly deepen the sense of connection.

The Importance of Being Present

Being emotionally present allows partners to build trust and safety, which are foundational to overcoming the trenches of distance often found in relationships plagued by insecure attachment styles.

- Building Trust: Consistent emotional presence shows reliability and commitment, reassuring partners that they are both valued and understood, which builds trust over time.
- Reducing Anxiety: For partners who may feel anxious or insecure, knowing that they are emotionally supported helps in alleviating fears of abandonment and rejection.
- Enhancing Connection: Emotional presence enriches interactions and deepens the connection, making the relationship more fulfilling for both individuals.

Challenges to Emotional Presence

Despite its benefits, achieving emotional presence can be challenging, particularly for those who have learned to protect themselves through emotional distance.

- Overcoming Personal Barriers: Individuals may need to confront and manage personal fears related to intimacy and vulnerability, often requiring them to deal with past traumas or ingrained defense mechanisms.
- Navigating Conflict: Learning to remain emotionally present during conflict, rather than withdrawing or shutting down, is crucial for maintaining intimacy during difficult conversations.
- Consistency in Effort: Emotional presence requires ongoing effort and commitment. It is not a one-time achievement but a continuous practice that needs nurturing.

Strategies for Cultivating Emotional Presence

Embracing emotional presence in a relationship involves practical steps and exercises that can foster intimacy and understanding.

- Mindfulness Practices: Engaging in mindfulness can enhance one's ability to remain present during interactions, helping individuals observe their emotions without judgment and stay engaged with their partner.
- Communication Skills Training: Partners can benefit from learning communication techniques that emphasize active listening, empathy, and validating each other's experiences.
- Therapeutic Support: Therapy can provide valuable tools and insights for overcoming barriers to emotional presence, especially for those with deep-rooted avoidant behaviors or anxiety around intimacy.

Embracing emotional presence is a transformative step from the isolation of distance to the warmth of intimacy. As couples learn to be present with each other's emotions, they lay down the bricks to bridge the gap in their relationship, paving the way for a deeper and more satisfying connection. This foundational practice sets the stage for further growth in commitment and vulnerability, topics that will be explored in the continuing sections of this chapter.

Commitment: Rewriting the Script of Retreat

For individuals with a history of avoidant attachment, commitment can feel like an anathema. The tendency to retreat at the first sign of emotional demand can be deeply ingrained, making the notion of commitment a formidable challenge. However, rewriting this script of retreat is essential for building lasting and fulfilling relationships. This section explores how individuals can redefine their understanding of commitment, moving beyond their fears to embrace a more connected and secure partnership.

Understanding the Fear of Commitment

At the heart of avoidant behavior is a fear that commitment will lead to loss—loss of independence, loss of identity, or being trapped in a relationship that might cause emotional pain. This fear often manifests as a script of retreat:

- Emotional Withdrawal: Pulling away emotionally whenever the relationship requires a deeper engagement or shows signs of serious commitment.
- Sabotage: Subconsciously undermining the relationship as it begins to demand more commitment.
- Avoidance of Future Planning: Reluctance to discuss or make plans for the future together as a way to keep the relationship in a state of ambiguity.

Redefining Commitment

Commitment in a relationship does not have to signify loss of freedom. Instead, it can be reframed as a pathway to greater emotional richness and stability—a state that actually enhances personal freedom by providing a reliable foundation from which both partners can grow.

- Security Over Constraint: Viewing commitment as a source of security rather than a constraint. A committed relationship provides a stable base that supports personal and mutual growth.
- Interdependence: Recognizing that a healthy relationship involves a balance of give and take, where independence and intimacy coexist without threatening one another.

Steps to Rewriting the Script

Changing deeply ingrained avoidance behaviors requires conscious effort and often, a structured approach:

- Incremental Commitment: Start with small commitments and gradually increase the stakes as trust builds. This could be as simple as committing to a weekly date night, progressing to bigger decisions like planning a vacation together.
- Communicating Needs and Boundaries: Openly discussing fears and expectations about commitment can alleviate misunderstandings and help partners support each other effectively. Setting clear boundaries is also crucial to ensure that neither partner feels overwhelmed.
- Reflective Practices: Engaging in personal reflection or journaling can help individuals understand their responses to commitment, identifying triggers that cause them to retreat.

Building Trust Through Actions

Commitment is ultimately demonstrated through actions—not just big gestures, but the everyday actions that show partners they are a priority.

- Consistency: Being reliable in small ways builds trust over time, showing that commitment is not just a verbal promise but a lived reality.
- Reassurance: Regularly reassuring each other of their importance in your life helps to strengthen the bond, making the commitment feel safer and more rewarding for both partners.

Rewriting the script of retreat involves embracing the nuances of commitment and recognizing its value in creating a fulfilling relationship. As individuals learn to commit, not out of obligation but from a desire for deeper connection, they pave the way for a relationship that is not only enduring but also enriching. Moving forward, the next section, will explore how open, vulnerable communication is integral to cementing this new script of commitment and enhancing the intimacy within the relationship.

In Dialogue: Learning the Language of Vulnerability

As relationships deepen, the ability to communicate vulnerably becomes essential. For individuals accustomed to emotional distance, learning the language of vulnerability is akin to learning a new dialect of emotional expression. This section discusses the significance of vulnerability in dialogue, the challenges it poses for those with avoidant attachment styles, and practical strategies for enhancing vulnerability in communication.

The Importance of Vulnerable Communication

Vulnerability in communication involves openly sharing one's thoughts, feelings, and fears without self-censorship or defensiveness. It is the cornerstone of intimacy and trust in a relationship, allowing partners to truly see and understand each other on a deeper level.

- Deepening Connections: Vulnerability helps to deepen emotional connections, transforming superficial interactions into meaningful exchanges.
- Building Trust: When partners are open and vulnerable, it demonstrates trust and fosters a similar response in return, thereby reinforcing the relationship's foundation.
- Facilitating Emotional Support: Sharing vulnerabilities allows partners to support each other through challenges, reinforcing the partnership's strength and resilience.

Challenges to Vulnerable Communication

For those with a history of avoiding intimacy, vulnerable communication can be daunting. It requires navigating past fears and changing long-standing patterns of interaction.

- Fear of Exposure: Vulnerability can feel like exposing one's weakest points to potential hurt or manipulation.
- Equating Vulnerability with Weakness: Many avoidants have learned to equate emotional openness with weakness or liability, beliefs that can hinder open communication.
- Lack of Practice: Simply not having much practice in expressing emotions can make vulnerability particularly challenging.

Strategies for Enhancing Vulnerability

Developing a comfort with vulnerability is a gradual process that can be fostered through specific strategies:

- Small Steps: Begin with sharing small, less consequential vulnerabilities to build confidence in the safety of being open.
- Create a Safe Environment: Both partners can work to create a communication environment where vulnerability is met with support, not criticism or dismissal.
- Use Reflective Listening: When one partner shares vulnerably, the other should practice reflective listening—repeating back what was heard to confirm understanding before responding. This practice validates the speaker's feelings and intentions.
- Scheduled Check-Ins: Setting aside regular times to share thoughts and feelings can help make vulnerable communication a routine part of the relationship.

The Role of Empathy

Empathy is critical in vulnerable dialogues as it allows each partner to not just hear but feel what the other is expressing. This emotional resonance can help soothe fears and build a bridge over previous emotional distances.

- Empathic Responses: Rather than offering solutions or dismissing concerns, responding with empathy to a partner's vulnerability encourages more open and honest communication.
- Cultivating Emotional Intelligence: Enhancing one's ability to recognize and respond to emotions can greatly improve empathic interactions between partners.

Learning the language of vulnerability transforms relationships by breaking down walls of emotional distance and building bridges of intimacy. As couples practice and become more comfortable with open, vulnerable communication, they find their relationship enriched with a deeper understanding and connection. This ongoing dialogue of vulnerability not only cements their commitment but also paves the way for a lasting, mutually supportive partnership.

Moving forward, Chapter 6, "The Internal Compass," will further dissect how individuals with avoidant attachment manage their internal defenses. We will explore how the internal dialogue of an avoidant individual impacts their external reality, providing deeper insights into the self-protective mechanisms that govern their interactions and relationships. This exploration is essential for anyone looking to understand and alter the deeply ingrained patterns that dictate avoidant behavior.

Chapter 5 Summary

The journey from emotional distance to intimacy in relationships, especially for those with avoidant or anxious attachment styles, involves embracing emotional presence. This requires more than physical closeness; it includes active listening, empathetic engagement, and meaningful nonverbal communication to foster deeper connections. Emotional presence helps build trust, reduces anxiety, and strengthens relationships.

However, achieving this presence faces challenges such as personal barriers to intimacy and conflict management. Practicing mindfulness, improving communication skills, and therapeutic support are key strategies for overcoming these barriers and cultivating emotional presence.

Additionally, commitment can be daunting for those with avoidant attachments, often seen as a threat to independence. By reframing commitment as a source of security and interdependence, and using strategies like incremental commitment and clear communication of needs and boundaries, individuals can begin to see it as supportive rather than restrictive.

Vulnerability in communication is also vital for deepening relationships. For those used to emotional distance, learning to express vulnerability without fear is challenging but necessary. Strategies such as taking small steps, creating a safe communication environment, and using reflective listening can enhance vulnerability and empathy, which are crucial for building trust and intimacy.

Together, these strategies help transform relationships from distant to intimately connected, laying the groundwork for ongoing growth in intimacy and commitment. This process not only enriches personal relationships but also sets the stage for exploring deeper dynamics in future interactions.

MY NOTES

Part III

Building Skills

for

Lasting Relationships

Chapter 6

The Internal Compass

Dissecting Avoidant Defenses: From Internal Dialogue to External Reality

In the journey towards understanding and reshaping attachment styles, particularly the avoidant type, it is crucial to examine the internal defenses that these individuals deploy. This chapter delves into the internal dialogues that often dictate the avoidant's interactions and how these thought patterns manifest in their external reality, influencing their behaviors and relationships.

Understanding Avoidant Defenses

Avoidant defenses are psychological mechanisms that protect individuals from perceived threats to their autonomy and emotional well-being. These defenses are often deeply rooted in early experiences where emotional expression was discouraged or went unvalidated. In adulthood, these defenses manifest as a series of internal dialogues that guide how avoidants perceive and react to intimacy and dependence.

- Minimization of Emotional Needs: A common internal dialogue among avoidants involves downplaying their emotional needs. This minimization serves as a defense against the vulnerability that comes with acknowledging and expressing these needs.

- Rationalization of Isolation: Avoidants often rationalize their preference for isolation with thoughts like, "I am better off alone" or "Relationships are too complicated." This rationalization helps justify their withdrawal from close emotional contacts.

- Dismissing the Importance of Relationships: Internally, avoidants may convince themselves that relationships and emotional connections are not essential for their happiness or success, thus fortifying their emotional barriers.

The Transition from Internal Dialogue to External Behavior

The internal dialogues of an avoidant significantly influence their external behaviors in relationships. Understanding this transition can help in identifying and modifying maladaptive patterns.

- Withdrawal Actions: The internal belief in the sufficiency of solitude translates into behaviors such as avoiding deep conversations, pulling away when things get emotionally intense, or even ending relationships prematurely.

- Control Over Emotional Expressions: The fear of emotional vulnerability can lead avoidants to carefully control and limit their emotional expressions. They might appear stoic or indifferent, even during emotionally charged situations.

- Selective Engagement: Reflecting their internal dialogues, avoidants might engage selectively in relationships, choosing partners who respect their need for distance or those who are unlikely to demand emotional depth.

Strategies to Modify Avoidant Defenses

Breaking down and modifying these ingrained defensive mechanisms requires conscious effort.

- Increasing Self-Awareness: Through self-reflection and possibly therapy, avoidants can become more aware of their defensive patterns and the internal dialogues that drive them. Journaling and mindfulness practices are useful tools for enhancing self-awareness.
- Challenging Internal Dialogues: Cognitive-behavioral therapy (CBT) techniques, such as thought challenging and restructuring, can help in modifying the negative beliefs that underpin avoidant behaviors.
- Practicing Vulnerability: Gradually exposing themselves to vulnerability in safe and controlled environments can help avoidants reduce their reliance on defensive mechanisms. This could involve sharing small personal things with trusted individuals or engaging in group therapy settings.

Cultivating Healthier Relationship Patterns

As avoidants work on understanding and adjusting their internal compass, they can begin to foster healthier ways of relating that do not rely solely on independence and emotional distance.

- Embracing Interdependence: Learning to see interdependence as a strength rather than a threat is key. This involves acknowledging that healthy relationships can enhance personal freedom rather than diminish it.
- Building Emotional Resilience: Developing tools for better emotional regulation and resilience helps in managing the discomfort that comes with increased intimacy.

- Enhancing Communication Skills: Effective communication is critical in altering avoidant patterns. Practicing openness, and learning to express needs and desires clearly, can improve relationship dynamics significantly.

Dissecting and understanding the internal dialogues and defenses of avoidant attachment is a crucial step towards developing a healthier internal compass. This progress paves the way for more genuine and fulfilling interactions, moving from a life of emotional solitude to one of rich, interconnected relationships.

Introspection: The Pathway to Inner Alignment

Introspection stands as a crucial practice for anyone, particularly individuals with avoidant attachment styles, aiming to understand and adjust their habitual ways of thinking and relating to others. This section explores how introspection serves as a vital pathway to achieving inner alignment, facilitating a deeper understanding of oneself and enhancing personal growth.

The Role of Introspection in Personal Growth

Introspection involves examining one's own thoughts, emotions, and behaviors in a reflective and deliberate manner. For those with avoidant attachment, introspection can be particularly transformative, allowing them to:

- Identify Underlying Fears: Many avoidants operate under surface-level motivations that mask deeper fears, such as fear of rejection or intimacy. Through introspection, these underlying fears can be uncovered and directly addressed.
- Recognize Patterns of Avoidance: Introspection helps individuals identify the specific situations or behaviors that trigger their avoidance mechanisms,

offering insight into how these patterns have developed and been maintained over time.

- Assess Personal Values and Beliefs: Often, avoidants may hold beliefs about relationships and independence that are misaligned with their deeper desires or needs. Introspection allows for a reevaluation of these beliefs in light of personal values and long-term goals.

Techniques for Effective Introspection

Effective introspection requires more than casual reflection; it involves structured techniques that promote a deeper understanding of oneself:

- Journaling: Writing down thoughts and feelings regularly can help clarify internal experiences and track changes over time. This practice can be particularly helpful in recognizing recurring themes or shifts in perception.
- Meditation and Mindfulness: These practices enhance present-moment awareness, making it easier to observe one's thought processes without immediate reaction or judgment. Meditation can provide the mental space needed to explore complex emotional landscapes.

Overcoming Challenges in Introspection

While introspection is a valuable tool for personal growth, individuals with avoidant attachment may face specific challenges in engaging with this practice:

- Resistance to Facing Uncomfortable Truths: Avoidants may initially resist introspection due to discomfort with the emotions or memories it can surface. Gradually approaching sensitive topics can help mitigate this resistance.

- Bias in Self-Perception: There is a tendency to have a skewed perception of oneself that either overemphasizes independence or underestimates the impact of avoidance on relationships. Objective measures, such as feedback from trusted friends or therapists, can provide a more balanced view.
- Maintaining Consistency: Regular introspective practice can be difficult to maintain, especially when life gets busy or emotional challenges arise. Setting a regular schedule or integrating introspection into daily routines can help sustain this practice.

The Benefits of Aligned Self-Understanding

As avoidant individuals deepen their self-understanding through introspection, they often discover a more aligned sense of self. This alignment can lead to:

- Improved Relationships: A clearer understanding of one's own needs and fears makes it easier to communicate and negotiate within relationships.
- Enhanced Emotional Regulation: Recognizing what triggers negative emotions or withdrawal allows individuals to develop more effective coping strategies.
- Greater Authenticity: Living in a way that reflects true personal values and desires leads to a more authentic and fulfilling life.

Through introspection, individuals with avoidant attachment can begin to dismantle the protective barriers they have built around their emotions, paving the way for a more engaged and emotionally rich life. This process of inner alignment is essential not only for personal happiness but also for the health and vitality of one's relationships. As introspection fosters a deeper connection with oneself, it sets the stage for the next step in personal development: enhancing self-compassion and understanding, which are vital for fully engaging in close, intimate relationships.

The Role of Self-Compassion in Overcoming Self-Sabotage

Self-sabotage in individuals with avoidant attachment often arises from deeply ingrained patterns of self-criticism and fear of intimacy. Self-compassion is a crucial tool in mitigating these patterns, facilitating a kinder and more accepting relationship with oneself. This section explores the transformative power of self-compassion in overcoming self-sabotage and how it prepares individuals for deeper relational healing.

Understanding Self-Sabotage in Avoidant Attachment

Self-sabotage for avoidants can manifest as withdrawing from relationships at key moments, resisting emotional closeness, or engaging in behaviors that push others away. This often stems from an internal dialogue that undervalues their worthiness of intimacy and love.

- Fear-Driven Behaviors: Fear of vulnerability often leads to behaviors that undermine relationship progress, such as reluctance to commit or communicate openly.
- Critical Self-Assessment: Harsh self-judgment about one's need for emotional independence often perpetuates a cycle of isolation and relationship avoidance.

The Healing Role of Self-Compassion

Self-compassion involves treating oneself with the same kindness, concern, and support one would show to a good friend. It has three main components:

- Self-Kindness: Extending kindness and understanding to oneself rather than harsh judgment and self-criticism.

- Common Humanity: Recognizing that suffering and personal inadequacy are part of the shared human experience — something that we all go through rather than being something that happens to "me" alone.
- Mindfulness: Taking a balanced approach to negative emotions so that feelings are neither suppressed nor exaggerated.

Strategies to Cultivate Self-Compassion

Cultivating self-compassion can help avoidants interrupt the cycle of self-sabotage by fostering a more supportive internal environment.

- Mindfulness Meditation: Practices such as mindfulness meditation help in acknowledging and sitting with painful feelings without over-identifying with them, allowing for a more compassionate and objective self-view.
- Reframing Internal Dialogue: Actively challenging critical or demeaning thoughts about oneself and replacing them with messages of kindness and acceptance.
- Compassion Exercises: Engaging in exercises specifically designed to enhance self-compassion, like writing a letter to oneself from the perspective of a compassionate friend.

Integrating Self-Compassion into Daily Life

Regularly practicing self-compassion can transform how avoidants relate to themselves and others, fostering greater openness and reducing fears around intimacy.

- Daily Self-Compassion Reminders: Setting reminders to engage in self-compassion practices or to affirm positive qualities about oneself.

As self-compassion strengthens, it lays the groundwork for addressing the deeper roots of avoidant attachment, which often lie in one's early childhood experiences. This preparation is essential as we move into Chapter 7, "Reparenting the Self." In the next chapter, we will explore how the echoes of childhood experiences shape present attachments and how individuals can foster their secure base through the art of self-parenting. By healing past wounds with compassion and understanding, individuals can build a foundation for healthier, more secure attachments in their current relationships.

Chapter 6 Summary

Chapter 6 delves into the internal defenses of individuals with avoidant attachment styles, exploring how their internal dialogues shape external behaviors and impact relationships. These defenses originate from early experiences where emotional expression was discouraged, leading to behaviors like minimizing emotional needs, rationalizing isolation, and dismissing relationships.

The chapter outlines strategies to modify these defenses, such as increasing self-awareness through journaling and mindfulness, challenging negative internal dialogues using cognitive-behavioral therapy techniques, and practicing vulnerability in controlled environments.

The discussion extends to how these internal mechanisms influence avoidant behaviors, such as withdrawal during emotional closeness and selective engagement in relationships. To cultivate healthier relationship patterns, the chapter suggests embracing interdependence, building emotional resilience, and enhancing communication skills. This shift aims to help individuals with avoidant attachment forge deeper and more meaningful connections by redefining their views on independence and emotional intimacy.

Overall, the chapter provides a roadmap for transforming avoidant defenses into healthier interpersonal engagement, facilitating personal growth and richer relationships.

MY NOTES

Chapter 7

Reparenting the Self

The Echoes of Childhood: How Past Parenting Influences Present Attachments

Understanding the impact of childhood experiences on adult attachment styles is crucial for personal development and healing. For those with avoidant attachment, reparenting the self is a transformative process that involves revisiting and understanding the influence of one's early parenting. This section delves into how childhood experiences shape adult relationships and how individuals can begin the journey of reparenting themselves to foster healthier, more secure attachments.

Impact of Childhood Experiences

The attachment patterns we exhibit as adults are often a reflection of our earliest experiences with caregivers. These foundational relationships teach us what to expect from others and how to interact in intimate relationships.

- Inconsistency and Emotional Unavailability: For many with avoidant attachment, childhood was marked by caregivers who were emotionally unavailable or inconsistently available. This unpredictability can lead to the development of self-reliance as a coping mechanism.
- Dismissal of Emotional Needs: If emotional expressions were dismissed or discouraged during childhood, children learn to suppress their feelings and needs, carrying this behavior into adulthood.

- Modeling of Independence: Caregivers who emphasized independence and minimized the importance of emotional support might foster the belief in children that seeking help or forming deep emotional connections is a sign of weakness.

The Concept of Reparenting

Reparenting involves taking steps to give oneself the care, affirmation, and emotional nurturing that may not have been adequately received in childhood. This process helps to heal old wounds and build the foundation for secure attachment.

- Understanding Needs: The first step in reparenting is recognizing and acknowledging one's emotional and physical needs that were unmet in childhood.
- Providing What Was Missing: Reparenting means actively providing for oneself what was missing in one's upbringing. This could involve self-soothing techniques, affirmations, or creating routines that foster a sense of security and stability.

Steps to Begin Reparenting

The journey of reparenting is deeply personal and often challenging, requiring both commitment and patience. Here are some strategies to start this transformative process:

- Self-Reflection: Engaging in introspection or journaling to identify the specific needs that were not met during childhood and the ways in which these unmet needs currently manifest in relationships.
- Building a Support System: Establishing relationships with people who understand and support one's reparenting journey can reinforce the efforts to

change. This might include friends, family, or support groups who provide empathy and encouragement.

- Practicing Mindfulness: Incorporating mindfulness practices can enhance emotional awareness and regulation, helping one stay connected to present experiences rather than automatically reverting to old patterns.

Reparenting oneself is a powerful step towards breaking the cycle of avoidant attachment and moving towards healthier, more secure relationship dynamics. By addressing the echoes of childhood and actively working to meet their own emotional needs, individuals can pave the way for more fulfilling and resilient relationships. This groundwork is essential as we further explore the specific tools and practices of reparenting, such as fostering a secure base and utilizing transitional objects and spaces for healing, in the subsequent sections of this chapter.

The Art of Self-Parenting: Fostering Your Secure Base

Self-parenting is an essential component of the reparenting process, particularly for those who experienced insecure attachments in childhood. It involves adopting the role of both caring parent and receptive child to oneself, thereby cultivating a secure base from which one can explore the world and relationships confidently. This section explores the practical aspects of self-parenting and how it helps in developing a secure internal foundation.

Foundations of Self-Parenting

The goal of self-parenting is to create a secure base within oneself, offering the love, acceptance, and security that may not have been adequately provided in one's early life. This involves several key practices:

- Self-Acceptance: Embracing all aspects of oneself, including vulnerabilities and flaws, without judgment. Self-acceptance is the bedrock of self-parenting, allowing individuals to feel worthy of love and care.
- Consistent Self-Care: Engaging in regular self-care practices that nurture both physical and emotional well-being. This might include maintaining a healthy lifestyle, practicing relaxation techniques, and seeking enjoyable activities that reinforce a sense of joy and satisfaction.
- Emotional Regulation: Developing skills to manage emotions effectively, especially during times of stress or when facing triggers. This can involve techniques such as deep breathing, mindfulness, and meditation.

Techniques for Effective Self-Parenting

Implementing self-parenting requires practical techniques that can be integrated into daily life, helping to foster a sense of security and stability internally:

- Internal Dialogue: Cultivating a nurturing internal dialogue is crucial. This involves speaking to oneself with kindness and encouragement, especially in moments of self-doubt or criticism.
- Setting Healthy Boundaries: Just as a caring parent sets boundaries to protect and teach a child, setting personal boundaries is essential for self-care. This includes learning to say no, prioritizing one's own needs, and protecting oneself from harmful influences.
- Creating Rituals and Routines: Establishing daily or weekly rituals that provide comfort and stability can reinforce the secure base. Examples might include a morning routine, regular exercise, or dedicated time for reflection and relaxation.

Building a Secure Base

The secure base formed through self-parenting allows individuals to approach relationships and challenges from a place of strength and stability, rather than fear and avoidance:

- Exploring New Relationships: With a secure base, individuals feel safer exploring new relationships and deepening existing ones, knowing they have a solid emotional foundation to return to.
- Risk-Taking and Growth: A secure base enables more risk-taking in personal and professional areas because individuals feel supported internally. They are more likely to pursue opportunities for growth, even when there's a possibility of failure.
- Resilience in Adversity: The inner security and self-support foster resilience, helping individuals bounce back more quickly from setbacks or emotional hurts.

The practice of self-parenting transforms the internal landscape from one of scarcity and fear to one of abundance and confidence. As individuals learn to provide for themselves the care and support they may have lacked, they unlock the potential for more fulfilling and emotionally rich lives.

This approach to building an internal secure base is crucial as it naturally leads into the next aspect of reparenting oneself, which involves using transitional objects and spaces for healing. These tools can help solidify the gains made through self-parenting and further enhance one's ability to navigate life's challenges with resilience and grace.

Transitional Objects and Spaces: Tools for Healing

Transitional objects and spaces play a crucial role in the psychological development and healing processes, especially for those engaging in self-reparenting. Originally conceptualized in developmental psychology, transitional objects like comfort blankets or favorite toys in childhood serve as sources of comfort and security in the absence of the primary caregiver. In adult therapy, the concept extends to any material or symbolic object, as well as designated physical or psychological spaces, that help individuals transition from a state of dependency and insecurity to autonomy and emotional resilience. This section explores how adults can utilize transitional objects and spaces to support their journey of emotional healing and growth.

Understanding Transitional Objects and Spaces

Transitional objects and spaces for adults function as anchors, providing emotional comfort and a sense of safety that allows for the exploration of often painful emotions and memories with reduced anxiety:

- Transitional Objects: These can be tangible items such as a piece of jewelry from a loved one, a book that offers comfort, or even a particular type of music that soothes the soul. These objects carry emotional significance and help ground the individual during times of distress.
- Transitional Spaces: Spaces, whether physical like a particular room or corner of a home, or psychological spaces such as meditation, provide a safe environment where one can explore vulnerabilities without fear of judgment or external pressures.

The Role of Transitional Objects and Spaces in Healing

These tools assist in the healing process by providing consistency and comfort, essential for those who have experienced instability or emotional neglect in their relationships:

- Safety and Security: Just as a child's blanket offers reassurance, adult transitional objects and spaces provide a psychological safety net, enabling individuals to venture into and retreat from emotional challenges at their own pace.
- Symbolic Bridging: They act as bridges between the internal world of the individual and the external reality, helping integrate fragmented parts of the self that were dissociated or suppressed in response to past trauma.
- Facilitating Emotional Expression: Transitional objects and spaces can evoke and contain emotions that are too intense or overwhelming to confront directly, allowing for gradual processing.

Integrating Transitional Tools into Daily Life

To effectively incorporate transitional objects and spaces into the healing process, individuals can:

- Personalize Selection: Choose objects and identify spaces that genuinely resonate on a personal emotional level. This choice is deeply personal and should feel intuitively comforting.
- Regular Engagement: Regularly engage with these objects or spend time in these spaces to reinforce their role as sources of emotional stability and safety.
- Mindful Reflection: Use times with these transitional tools to practice mindfulness and reflect on personal growth and emotional challenges. This could involve journaling, deep breathing exercises, or simply sitting quietly with one's thoughts.

Creating Rituals

Developing rituals around transitional objects and spaces can enhance their effectiveness:

- Routine Interaction: Establish a routine that involves the transitional object or space, such as holding a cherished stone during daily meditation or retreating to a designated space while journaling or reflecting on the day's events.
- Rituals of Comfort: In moments of distress, use the object or space to perform comforting rituals—listening to a specific song, wrapping oneself in a particular blanket, or reading a favorite book can all be soothing practices.

The use of transitional objects and spaces is a powerful method in the toolkit of self-reparenting, offering tangible and symbolic support on the journey toward emotional healing. As individuals become more adept at utilizing these tools, they build stronger foundations of security and resilience, essential for navigating the complexities of adult relationships and personal growth. This foundation of resilience and self-comprehension is particularly valuable as we move into the next phase of emotional evolution. In Chapter 8, "The Metamorphosis," we will explore how endings, such as breakups or the conclusion of significant life phases, can serve as beginnings for new growth and the embrace of change, paving the way for the formation of new, healthier attachments.

Chapter 7 Summary

This section explores how childhood experiences shape adult attachment styles, particularly focusing on individuals with avoidant attachment and the transformative process of reparenting. This process involves revisiting early parenting influences and addressing the emotional neglect or inconsistency experienced.

Key to reparenting is understanding and meeting one's unmet emotional and physical needs from childhood. Techniques like self-reflection, building a supportive network, and practicing mindfulness are emphasized as methods to begin this healing journey.

Additionally, the chapter delves into self-parenting, a practice where individuals nurture their inner child to foster a secure base within themselves. This includes practices of self-acceptance, consistent self-care, and emotional regulation to cultivate a secure, internal foundation that promotes healthier relationships and personal growth. Effective self-parenting involves adopting a nurturing internal dialogue, setting healthy boundaries, and creating comforting rituals and routines.

The concept of transitional objects and spaces is also introduced as tools for emotional healing and growth. These objects and spaces serve as emotional anchors that provide comfort and security, facilitating a safer exploration of vulnerabilities and enhancing the individual's capacity for emotional resilience.

Overall, this chapter provides a comprehensive guide on how individuals can heal from past traumas, build a secure internal foundation, and pave the way for more fulfilling relationships and personal development through the practices of reparenting and self-parenting.

MY NOTES

Chapter 8

The Metamorphosis

Endings as Beginnings: Perspectives on Breakups

The end of a significant relationship often marks a pivotal moment in one's personal journey, serving as both an ending and a beginning. For those who have engaged in the deep work of self-reparenting and healing, breakups can be reframed from purely painful experiences to opportunities for profound personal growth and transformation. This section explores how endings can be viewed as beginnings, allowing individuals to emerge stronger and more self-aware.

Reframing the Experience of Breakups

The pain of a breakup can be overwhelming, but it also presents a unique opportunity to apply the lessons learned from past relationships and from the process of self-reparenting.

- Opportunity for Self-Reflection: A breakup often prompts deep introspection about what one truly wants and needs in a relationship. It provides a chance to reassess personal values, desires, and the non-negotiable aspects of one's relational life.
- Clarification of Boundaries: Endings can highlight the boundaries that were not effectively upheld and provide clarity on the boundaries that need to be more firmly established in future relationships.

- Strength and Resilience: Surviving and growing from the pain of a breakup can reinforce an individual's resilience, proving to themselves that they can handle adversity and emerge stronger.

Learning from the Loss

Every relationship provides valuable lessons about love, compatibility, conflict resolution, and personal limits. A breakup is a critical time to harvest these lessons:

- Understanding Patterns: Reflecting on the relationship can help identify any recurring patterns that may be contributing to relationship failures. This could include tendencies to choose certain types of partners or to react in specific ways to relationship stress.
- Emotional Growth: Processing the emotions that arise from a breakup can lead to greater emotional maturity, including better management of feelings like grief, anger, and loneliness.

Growth After Goodbye

The post-breakup period can be a powerful phase of personal growth and self-discovery.

- Investment in Self: With more free emotional and physical space, individuals can invest in areas of life that were previously neglected. This might include personal hobbies, career ambitions, or new relationships.
- Expanding Social Networks: Breakups often prompt the expansion of social networks, as individuals reach out for support or engage in new activities and communities.
- Revisiting Personal Goals: Without the compromise that relationships often require, one can more freely pursue personal goals and dreams that were on hold.

Practical Steps for Transformative Healing

To truly transform a breakup into a beginning, practical steps can be undertaken to ensure healthy processing and growth:

- Structured Reflection: Setting aside time for structured reflection through journaling or therapy can facilitate the extraction of insights from the relationship and breakup experience.
- Self-Care Practices: Engaging in self-care practices that nurture both body and mind is crucial. This might include regular exercise, healthy eating, mindfulness meditation, or simply ensuring adequate rest.
- Seeking Support: Leaning on friends, family, or professionals for support not only helps in processing the breakup but also in rebuilding one's sense of worth and belonging.

Viewing breakups as opportunities for growth encourages a shift in perspective that aligns with the ongoing journey of self-reparenting and emotional maturation. This approach allows individuals to transform their most challenging moments into catalysts for change and development, setting the stage for future relationships that are healthier and more aligned with their evolved selves. As we continue to explore the themes of metamorphosis, the subsequent sections will delve deeper into how personal transformations post-separation can lead to a reawakening and the embrace of new changes and attachments.

Growth After Goodbye: Transformation Post-Separation

Navigating the aftermath of a relationship breakup can be a profound journey of self-discovery and personal growth. While the initial phases of a breakup are often filled with emotional turmoil, the period following the separation offers a unique opportunity for transformative growth. This section examines the potential for personal evolution post-breakup and how individuals can leverage this challenging time to foster significant changes in their lives.

Embracing the Opportunity for Self-Discovery

A breakup disrupts the status quo and compels individuals to reflect on their identity outside of the relational context. This disruption can serve as a powerful catalyst for self-discovery:

- Reassessment of Self-Identity: Post-separation is an ideal time for individuals to explore aspects of their identity that might have been overshadowed or suppressed within the relationship. This can include revisiting old interests, exploring new hobbies, or even changing career paths.
- Increased Self-Reliance: Without a partner to lean on, individuals often develop stronger self-reliance, discovering their capabilities and strengths that may not have been apparent while in the relationship.

Leveraging Pain for Growth

The pain experienced during a breakup, while challenging, can also be a profound teacher:

- Learning from Emotional Vulnerability: The emotional vulnerability exposed by a breakup can teach resilience and emotional regulation skills. Embracing these feelings rather than suppressing them can lead to deeper emotional intelligence.

- Insights into Relationship Dynamics: Reflecting on the relationship's dynamics can provide valuable insights into personal relationship patterns, needs, and areas for improvement.

Strategies for Facilitating Growth Post-Breakup

To capitalize on the growth opportunities presented by a breakup, several strategies can be employed:

- Setting New Goals: Post-breakup is an opportune time to set new personal and professional goals. These goals can provide direction and a sense of purpose that might have been lost.
- Expanding Social Connections: Building or strengthening connections with friends, family, and new acquaintances can provide emotional support and new perspectives.
- Engaging in Professional Development: Investing time and energy into professional growth not only distracts from the pain of the breakup but also boosts self-esteem and future prospects.

Implementing Change through Routine and Ritual

Establishing new routines and rituals is essential for implementing and sustaining the changes begun during the post-separation period:

- Healthy Routines: Establishing routines that promote physical health, such as exercise and nutrition, can also enhance mental health.
- Rituals of Self-Care: Creating rituals around self-care, such as regular mindfulness practice or journaling, can help maintain emotional balance and reinforce a positive self-image.

Future-Oriented Thinking

Adopting a future-oriented perspective helps individuals move from focusing on what has been lost to what can be gained:

- Visualization Techniques: Regularly visualizing a positive future can motivate individuals to take actionable steps toward making that future a reality.
- Openness to New Relationships: While there might be a natural hesitancy to form new romantic connections, staying open to new relationships is crucial. These relationships can be approached with fresh perspectives and insights gained from the post-breakup growth.

As individuals navigate the transformative period post-separation, they not only recover from their loss but also can achieve significant personal development that reshapes their approach to relationships and life. This journey of growth after goodbye is a critical step towards the reawakening of one's desires and capacities, leading into the next phase of embracing change and forming new, healthier attachments, as discussed in the upcoming sections of "The Reawakening: Embracing Change and New Attachments."

The Reawakening: Embracing Change and New Attachments

After navigating the often-turbulent waters of a breakup and the subsequent period of personal growth, individuals find themselves at a threshold of reawakening—an opportunity to embrace change positively and form new, healthier attachments. This section explores how individuals can open themselves to new experiences and relationships, integrating the lessons learned from past experiences to create a fulfilling future.

The Concept of Reawakening

Reawakening refers to the revitalization of one's emotional life, a rebirth that follows the introspection and personal development triggered by significant life changes. It involves:

- Renewed Sense of Self: Embracing an evolved identity that reflects the depth of personal growth achieved, recognizing new strengths, and acknowledging changes in personal values and desires.
- New Perspectives on Relationships: Adopting fresh approaches to relationships that incorporate greater self-awareness and understanding of one's needs and boundaries.

Embracing Change

Change is constant, but embracing it after a period of personal transformation involves a conscious choice to see change as an opportunity rather than a threat.

- Flexibility and Openness: Remaining flexible and open to new experiences allows for the exploration of different aspects of life and forming new connections.
- Letting Go of the Past: Actively working to release old patterns and emotional baggage to make room for new relationships and opportunities.

Forming New Attachments

Forming new attachments involves both caution and courage, applying lessons from past relationships to establish healthier dynamics in new ones.

- Applying Lessons Learned: Using insights from previous experiences to build healthier relationship dynamics.

- Choosing Differently: Consciously selecting partners who align with one's current values and life goals.
- Building Trust Gradually: Allowing relationships to develop naturally through shared experiences and consistent, reliable actions.

Strategies for Navigating New Relationships

To ensure that new relationships are built on a healthy foundation, certain strategies can be particularly effective:

- Communication Skills: Engaging in open and honest communication from the outset, setting a precedent for transparency and mutual respect.
- Emotional Availability: Being fully present in interactions to foster deep and meaningful connections.
- Continuous Self-awareness: Maintaining an ongoing practice of self-awareness to manage personal behaviors and emotional responses effectively.

The Role of Personal Support Systems

Developing and maintaining a strong personal support system is vital as one explores new relationships and experiences.

- Leveraging Community Resources: Engaging with community resources such as support groups or workshops that focus on personal development and emotional health.
- Building a Network of Support: Cultivating a network of friends and family who provide emotional support and practical advice.

As individuals embark on this journey of reawakening, they not only reshape their personal lives but also bring new vitality to all their relationships. This process of embracing change and forming new attachments lays the groundwork for ongoing personal evolution, enhancing individual well-being and enriching the broader community. This reawakening sets the stage for the next chapter, Chapter 9: Rebuilding the Self, where we will delve deeper into how individuals reconstruct their identity and self-concept after significant transformations, furthering their journey towards a fully realized and autonomous self.

Chapter 8 Summary

Chapter 8, "The Metamorphosis," explores the transformative potential of breakups, viewing them not just as endings but as significant opportunities for personal growth and self-discovery. It reframes the experience of breakups as a chance for deep introspection and self-reflection, allowing individuals to reassess their personal values, clarify boundaries, and strengthen resilience. This perspective encourages seeing each relationship as a learning experience, providing valuable lessons on love, compatibility, and personal limits.

The chapter outlines practical steps for leveraging a breakup for transformative healing, including structured reflection, engaging in self-care practices, and seeking support from friends, family, or professionals. It discusses the post-breakup period as a pivotal time for personal growth, where individuals can invest in neglected areas of their lives, expand their social networks, and revisit personal goals.

Additionally, it covers the concept of reawakening, where individuals embrace change and form new, healthier attachments post-breakup. This includes adopting new perspectives on relationships, building trust gradually, and maintaining a strong personal support system.

Overall, "The Metamorphosis" presents breakups as catalysts for profound personal development and reawakening, setting the stage for future relationships that are more aligned with one's evolved self.

MY NOTES

Part IV

Establishing
and Maintaining
Secure Attachments

Chapter 9

Rebuilding the Self

Unearthing the Wounded Self: A Journey to Recovery

In the aftermath of significant life changes and personal evolution, individuals often face the challenge of confronting and healing the deeper, perhaps long-buried aspects of their psyche. This process, essential for true recovery and growth, involves unearthing the wounded self—those parts affected by past traumas, unresolved conflicts, and neglected needs. Chapter 9 begins with exploring how to recognize and recover these vulnerable segments of the self, setting the stage for a comprehensive and lasting transformation.

Identifying the Wounded Self

The wounded self consists of those aspects of an individual's identity that have been hurt, neglected, or repressed over the years. This can include emotional wounds from childhood, painful experiences in relationships, or traumas from any stage of life. Recognizing the wounded self involves:

- Awareness of Emotional Triggers: Noticing what situations, comments, or behaviors trigger disproportionate emotional reactions can help identify the aspects of the self that are still hurting.
- Reflection on Past Relationships: Analyzing patterns in past relationships can reveal recurring themes and wounds that need healing.
- Engagement with Inner Dialogue: Listening to one's internal conversations can uncover self-critical or self-demeaning thoughts that signal areas of unresolved emotional pain.

Approaches to Healing

Once the wounded self is identified, the process of healing can begin. This journey requires courage, commitment, and often, the support of therapeutic interventions.

- Therapeutic Methods: Engaging with psychological therapies such as cognitive-behavioral therapy (CBT), psychoanalysis, or trauma-informed therapies can provide structured ways to deal with emotional wounds.
- Self-Compassion Practices: Developing a practice of self-compassion is crucial in healing the wounded self. This might involve self-kindness, recognizing the universality of suffering, and mindfulness.
- Revisiting and Recontextualizing Memories: Therapeutically revisiting painful memories with a professional can help to recontextualize those experiences and reduce their emotional hold.

Building a Supportive Environment

Creating an environment that supports recovery is essential for anyone on the path to healing their wounded self.

- Cultivating Healthy Relationships: Establishing and maintaining relationships that are nurturing and supportive can provide the emotional safety needed for recovery.
- Community Involvement: Engaging with community groups or finding support networks focused on healing and personal development can reinforce the individual's efforts and provide valuable resources.
- Routine of Wellness: Integrating routines that promote physical, mental, and emotional well-being—such as regular exercise, balanced nutrition, and meditation—can support overall health and fortify the individual during the healing process.

Transforming Pain into Strength

As individuals work through the layers of their wounded self, they often discover an inner strength and resilience they might not have recognized before. This transformation involves:

- Empowering Self-Discovery: Through the process of healing, individuals often uncover strengths, talents, and capacities previously overshadowed by their wounds.
- Reframing the Narrative: Shifting the personal narrative from one of victimhood to one of survival and empowerment can change how individuals perceive themselves and their life stories.
- Integrating the Lessons: Incorporating the lessons learned from the journey of healing into daily life ensures that the growth and changes are sustained.

The journey to recover the wounded self is both challenging and profoundly rewarding. It not only heals past pains but also facilitates a reengagement with life that is more vibrant and whole. This process of rebuilding the self is instrumental in paving the way for the next chapter, where individuals learn to consolidate their newfound insights and strengths into a cohesive identity, continuing their path towards full personal actualization and empowerment.

The Stages of Healing: From Acknowledgment to Action

Healing from emotional wounds is a journey that typically unfolds in stages, from the initial acknowledgment of the pain to active steps toward recovery and transformation. Understanding these stages can provide a roadmap for those on the path to healing, helping to manage expectations and measure progress. This section outlines these crucial stages and offers guidance on navigating each one effectively.

Stage 1: Acknowledgment

The first step in the healing process is acknowledging that there is a wound. This involves recognizing the sources of pain, whether they stem from childhood experiences, traumatic events, or dysfunctional relationships.

- Recognition: Identifying the pain points and their origins is crucial. This may require reflective practices such as journaling, meditation, or discussions in therapy.
- Acceptance: Accepting that these experiences have impacted one's life and that healing is necessary is a vital part of this stage.

Stage 2: Understanding

With acknowledgment comes the need to understand how these wounds have influenced one's behavior, relationships, and self-perception.

- Connecting the Dots: Analyzing how past pain has shaped current thinking and behavior patterns. This might involve exploring triggers and the defense mechanisms that have developed over time.
- Educational Insight: Learning about psychological concepts and attachment theories can provide insights into one's behaviors and choices.

Stage 3: Processing

Processing the emotional content of one's wounds is often the most challenging part of healing. It involves confronting and working through the pain, rather than avoiding it.

- Emotional Expression: Allowing oneself to feel and express the emotions associated with the wounds. This could be through therapy, creative expression, or safe and supportive interpersonal connections.
- Therapeutic Interventions: Engaging with professional help to safely process these emotions. Techniques may include talk therapy, EMDR (Eye Movement Desensitization and Reprocessing), art therapy, or group therapy.

Stage 4: Integration

Integration involves assimilating the healed aspects of oneself into a coherent whole, recognizing that past experiences are part of one's story but do not define it.

- Rebuilding Identity: Constructing a new, healthier identity that includes but is not overshadowed by past wounds.

- Incorporating Lessons Learned: Applying the insights gained from the healing process to enhance personal growth and improve how one relates to others.

Stage 5: Action

The final stage is about taking proactive steps to live out the changes that have occurred internally, ensuring that healing translates into tangible improvements in daily life.

- Making Changes: Implementing practical changes in one's life based on the healing achieved. This could involve setting new boundaries, changing relationship dynamics, or pursuing new goals that were previously hindered by unhealed wounds.
- Maintenance and Resilience: Developing routines and practices that maintain emotional health and build resilience against future stresses.

Moving Forward

As individuals progress through these stages, they gradually build a foundation of emotional health that supports a more engaged and fulfilling life. The process of moving from acknowledgment to action is not linear and might require revisiting certain stages as new layers of understanding or challenges emerge.

This structured approach to healing is crucial as it prepares individuals for the next chapter in their journey—continuing their development and solidifying their renewed sense of self. The transformation witnessed through these stages not only enhances personal well-being but also enriches relationships and professional endeavors, leading to a more integrated and authentic life experience.

Reconstructing Identity Beyond Attachment Styles

In the journey of self-discovery and healing, reconstructing one's identity beyond the confines of attachment styles is a pivotal step. This process involves redefining who one is independent of the patterns that have historically dictated emotional responses and interactions. By understanding and reshaping these aspects of the self, individuals can forge a more authentic and empowered identity.

Understanding the Influence of Attachment Styles

Attachment styles, formed early in life, profoundly influence how individuals perceive themselves and interact in relationships. Recognizing these styles is just the beginning:

- Awareness: Identifying how specific attachment styles influence one's behavior and relationships is crucial. This may involve recognizing tendencies towards avoidance, anxiety, or disorganized behaviors.
- Decoupling Self-Identity from Attachment: Individuals often define themselves based on their relational patterns. Detaching from these definitions allows for a broader understanding of the self beyond relational dynamics.

Strategies for Identity Reconstruction

Reconstructing identity involves several strategic approaches that foster a deeper, more comprehensive sense of self that transcends past conditioning.

- Integrative Self-Reflection: Engaging in practices that promote self-reflection and introspection can help individuals explore and integrate various aspects of their personality beyond their attachment tendencies.

- Expanding Self-Concept: Activities and experiences that challenge existing self-concepts — such as new hobbies, travel, or professional roles — can help reshape how one views oneself.
- Consistent Self-Expression: Authentic self-expression in various contexts reinforces the reconstructed identity and helps solidify changes in self-perception.

Embracing a Holistic Self-View

Developing a holistic view of oneself that includes but is not limited to attachment styles is essential for sustained personal growth.

- Balanced Attributes: Recognizing and developing a range of attributes and qualities that reflect one's true self, such as resilience, creativity, empathy, and intelligence.
- Self-Acceptance: Embracing all parts of oneself, including imperfections and past mistakes, as integral components of one's identity.
- Cultivating Inner Values: Aligning daily actions and decisions with core values and beliefs strengthens the reconstructed identity and ensures it is deeply rooted in what truly matters to the individual.

Living Out the New Identity

As the new, more integrated identity takes shape, living it out in everyday life is the final, ongoing phase of reconstruction.

- Consistency in Behavior: Ensuring that actions and interactions consistently reflect the new identity helps reinforce and validate the changes.
- Adaptive Growth: Being open to continual growth and adaptation as life circumstances change ensures that the identity remains dynamic and relevant.

Preparing for Continued Evolution

The process of reconstructing identity is not a finite one; it is a continuous journey that evolves as individuals grow and their life contexts change. This ongoing evolution prepares one for the next stages of personal development, where deeper explorations of self and further enhancements in living a fulfilled life are pursued.

In the next chapter, "The Evolving Self," we will delve deeper into how this reconstructed identity facilitates ongoing personal development and adaptation. This includes exploring how individuals can maintain and nurture their growth, ensuring that their identity evolution positively impacts all areas of their life, from personal relationships to professional achievements.

Chapter 9 Summary

Chapter 9, "Rebuilding the Self," examines the process of confronting and healing the deeper, often long-buried aspects of one's psyche following significant life changes. It emphasizes the importance of unearthing the wounded self—parts of an individual's identity that have been affected by past traumas, unresolved conflicts, and neglected needs. This process involves identifying emotional triggers, reflecting on past relationships to uncover recurring themes, and engaging with one's inner dialogue to discover self-critical or demeaning thoughts.

The chapter outlines several approaches to healing, including therapeutic methods like cognitive-behavioral therapy, self-compassion practices, and revisiting painful memories to recontextualize them. Creating a supportive environment is crucial, which involves cultivating healthy relationships, engaging with community groups, and establishing routines that promote well-being.

As individuals work through their wounded aspects, they often discover newfound strength and resilience, reframing their personal narratives from victimhood to empowerment and integrating the lessons learned into their daily lives. This transformative journey not only fosters healing but also facilitates a reengagement with life that is richer and more integrated, setting the stage for future growth and more fulfilling relationships.

MY NOTES

Chapter 10

The Evolving Self

The Alchemy of Healing: Turning Pain into Empowerment

In the transformative journey of self-healing, one of the most profound shifts is the ability to transform pain into empowerment. This process, akin to alchemy, involves converting the raw elements of suffering and hardship into valuable insights and strengths. This chapter explores how individuals can harness their past adversities to foster resilience, increase self-awareness, and empower themselves to navigate life with renewed purpose and clarity.

Understanding the Transformative Potential of Pain

Painful experiences, while inherently challenging, hold the potential for significant personal growth. Recognizing this potential is the first step in the alchemical process:

- Pain as a Catalyst: Begin by viewing pain not as a barrier but as a catalyst for change. It often forces introspection and reevaluation of life paths, relationships, and self-identity.
- Learning from Adversity: Every challenge carries lessons about resilience, personal limits, boundaries, and our deepest values and needs.

Steps to Transform Pain into Empowerment

Transforming pain into empowerment involves several deliberate steps, each aimed at extracting wisdom and strength from difficult experiences:

1. Emotional Acknowledgment: Fully acknowledging and accepting the emotions associated with painful experiences is crucial. This means allowing oneself to feel and express feelings without judgment.
2. Insight Extraction: Reflect on the circumstances and outcomes of painful events. What did they teach about personal strength, vulnerabilities, or needs? How did they reshape understanding of personal and professional relationships?
3. Applied Learning: Use these insights to inform future decisions and interactions. This might mean setting stronger boundaries, pursuing new opportunities, or changing interaction patterns in relationships.

Building Resilience Through Self-Reflection

A key component of turning pain into empowerment is building resilience—the ability to recover from setbacks and adapt to change and difficulty:

- Develop Coping Strategies: Identify and cultivate coping strategies that have been effective in past challenges. Consider incorporating new strategies such as mindfulness, meditation, or physical activity to strengthen resilience.
- Create a Resilience Plan: Prepare for future stressors by developing a personal resilience plan that includes proactive steps for managing stress and emotional upheaval.

Fostering Continuous Growth and Learning

The journey of transforming pain does not end once immediate challenges are overcome. Continuous growth and adaptation are necessary to maintain and expand upon the gains made:

- Lifelong Learning Attitude: Embrace an attitude of lifelong learning, continuously seeking personal and professional development opportunities to enhance skills and knowledge.
- Adaptive Mindset: Stay open to reassessing and adjusting one's approach to life and relationships as circumstances change and new information becomes available.

Practical Application of Empowered Living

To truly live out the empowerment gained through this transformative process, consider the following applications:

- Assertive Living: Use the empowerment gained from past pain to live more assertively, ensuring that personal and professional decisions align with one's true self and values.
- Enhanced Interpersonal Relationships: Apply the insights from past experiences to improve how you engage in and nurture relationships, promoting healthier and more fulfilling interactions.

Turning pain into empowerment changes the narrative from one of victimhood to one of victory and growth. It involves not only overcoming the immediate effects of painful experiences but also integrating the lessons learned into everyday life to build a stronger, more resilient self. This ongoing process ensures that each individual is continually evolving, ready to meet future challenges with confidence and a deep understanding of their capabilities and worth.

As this chapter concludes, the journey of "The Evolving Self" continues, fostering a commitment to sustaining these changes and continuously exploring new pathways for personal and relational development, ensuring a lifelong trajectory of growth and fulfillment.

Cognitive-Behavioral Strategies: Reframing the Mindset

Cognitive-behavioral strategies are essential tools in the journey toward personal growth and healing, particularly in the context of transforming pain into empowerment. These strategies focus on identifying and changing negative thought patterns that can hinder progress, ultimately reframing one's mindset to support healthier, more adaptive ways of thinking and behaving. This section delves into practical cognitive-behavioral techniques that individuals can employ to actively reshape their mental landscape and enhance their overall well-being.

Understanding Cognitive-Behavioral Strategies

Cognitive-behavioral therapy (CBT) is based on the concept that our thoughts, feelings, and behaviors are interconnected, and that altering one can lead to changes in the others. This approach involves two main components:

- Cognitive Strategies: These involve recognizing and challenging negative or distorted thinking patterns and replacing them with more accurate and beneficial thoughts.
- Behavioral Strategies: These focus on changing behaviors through techniques such as exposure therapy, activity scheduling, and role-playing, which can alter emotional and cognitive states.

Key Cognitive-Behavioral Techniques

1. Thought Records: Thought records are a fundamental CBT technique that involves writing down negative thoughts, identifying the distortions in these thoughts, and then challenging them with more rational responses. This practice helps to clarify how certain thought patterns are influencing emotions and behaviors.

2. Mindfulness and Meditation: These practices cultivate a state of awareness and presence that can help individuals observe their thoughts without judgment, recognizing that thoughts are not facts and do not need to dictate emotional responses.

3. Reframing Techniques: Reframing involves changing the way a situation is perceived and thus changing one's emotional response to it. This could mean viewing a challenging situation not as a threat but as an opportunity to learn or demonstrate resilience.

4. Behavioral Activation: This strategy combats inertia and low motivation, common in depression and anxiety, by scheduling positive activities that are likely to generate pleasant experiences and improve mood.

Applying Cognitive-Behavioral Strategies in Everyday Life

To effectively use cognitive-behavioral strategies in daily life, consider the following applications:

- Routine Practice: Integrate cognitive-behavioral exercises into daily routines. For instance, start the day with a mindfulness session or end it with a thought record to assess and adjust thoughts throughout the day.

- Progressive Exposure: Gradually expose yourself to feared or avoided situations to decrease sensitivity and increase confidence. Start with less challenging situations and build up to more difficult ones.

- Self-Dialogue Enhancement: Regularly practice positive self-dialogue, especially during times of stress or when facing setbacks. Remind yourself of your strengths, past successes, and the irrational nature of negative thoughts.

Building a Cognitive-Behavioral Mindset

Developing a cognitive-behavioral mindset involves consistency and commitment to these practices:

- Education: Continuously educate yourself about cognitive distortions and behavioral economics to better understand how your mind processes information and how you might be unwittingly sabotaging your own happiness.
- Feedback Loops: Establish feedback loops with trusted friends, family, or a therapist who can help identify cognitive distortions and suggest alternative thoughts or behaviors.
- Journaling: Keep a journal to track thoughts, emotions, and behaviors over time. This can provide valuable insights into patterns that need to be addressed and serve as a record of progress.

Cognitive-behavioral strategies are powerful tools for anyone seeking to transform their mindset and overcome the challenges that have held them back. By systematically applying these techniques, individuals can actively foster a more positive, resilient, and adaptive mental state, laying a strong foundation for continued growth and success. As these strategies are integrated and become habitual, they pave the way for sustained improvements in emotional and psychological health, enhancing one's ability to navigate the complexities of life with greater ease and confidence.

Mindfulness and Acceptance: Anchors in the Emotional Storm

In the ongoing journey of self-transformation and healing, mindfulness and acceptance stand out as essential practices. These techniques serve as stable anchors in managing emotional turbulence, helping individuals to navigate the highs and lows of their internal experiences with greater ease and resilience. This section explores how integrating mindfulness and acceptance into daily life can significantly enhance emotional stability and foster a profound sense of peace.

Understanding Mindfulness and Acceptance

Mindfulness involves maintaining a moment-by-moment awareness of our thoughts, feelings, bodily sensations, and surrounding environment, often cultivated through meditation. Acceptance is closely related to mindfulness and involves acknowledging the realities of any given situation without trying to change or protest them. Together, these practices help individuals:

- Reduce Reactivity: By observing their thoughts and emotions without judgment, individuals can break the cycle of automatic, reflexive reactions to feelings of distress.
- Enhance Emotional Regulation: Regular mindfulness practice strengthens the ability to manage and respond to emotions in a balanced and reasoned manner.

Key Practices of Mindfulness and Acceptance

1. Daily Meditation: Setting aside time each day for meditation can help cultivate a baseline of calm and increase one's ability to remain centered during emotional upheavals.

2. Body Scans: This practice involves mentally scanning one's body for areas of tension and consciously releasing this tension. It helps to connect the mind and body, promoting overall relaxation.

3. Mindful Observation: Engaging fully with the present moment, whether it's while eating, walking, or talking, can help deepen one's sense of being grounded and reduce the tendency to ruminate on the past or worry about the future.

4. Acceptance Exercises: Actively practicing acceptance in situations that cannot be changed (e.g., during a traffic jam or when facing a chronic illness) can help decrease frustration and anxiety, shifting focus to actionable aspects of life.

Integrating Mindfulness and Acceptance into Everyday Life

To make mindfulness and acceptance part of daily life, consider the following strategies:

- Mindful Routines: Incorporate mindfulness into regular activities, like brushing teeth or washing dishes, to enhance presence and awareness throughout the day.
- Use of Apps and Guides: Utilize guided meditations through apps or online platforms to assist in developing a consistent mindfulness practice.
- Acceptance Affirmations: Regularly remind yourself of the power of acceptance with affirmations like, "I accept this moment as it is," or "I choose to respond with calm."

The Benefits of a Mindful and Accepting Approach

Adopting a mindful and accepting approach to life's challenges offers numerous benefits:

- Improved Mental Health: Reductions in stress, anxiety, and depressive symptoms are common outcomes for those who practice mindfulness and acceptance regularly.
- Enhanced Relationships: By responding to others with mindfulness and acceptance, individuals can improve communication and deepen connections, even in difficult circumstances.
- Greater Overall Well-Being: Cultivating mindfulness and acceptance often leads to greater life satisfaction, as individuals learn to appreciate the present and live more fully in each moment.

As individuals deepen their practice of mindfulness and acceptance, they prepare themselves for the next stage of personal growth, as discussed in Chapter 11, where these foundational practices help manage and navigate more complex emotional landscapes. This ongoing development is essential for maintaining emotional balance and building a life of sustained peace and fulfillment.

Chapter 10 Summary

Chapter 10, "The Evolving Self," explores the transformative power of pain and the process of converting it into empowerment and personal growth. This chapter outlines how recognizing the potential in painful experiences can catalyze self-reflection and learning, leading to significant personal development. It details steps to transform pain into empowerment, including fully acknowledging emotions, extracting insights from difficult experiences, and applying these lessons to enhance future resilience and decision-making.

Key to this transformation is building resilience through self-reflection, developing effective coping strategies, and creating a resilience plan for future challenges. The chapter emphasizes the importance of continuous growth and learning, encouraging an adaptive mindset and lifelong learning attitude to maintain and expand upon the gains made.

Practical applications of these concepts include living assertively to align decisions with one's true self and values, and applying insights from past pains to improve interpersonal relationships. This approach not only facilitates overcoming immediate challenges but also integrates the lessons learned into everyday life, building a stronger, more resilient self-capable of facing future challenges with confidence and deep self-awareness.

MY NOTES

Chapter 11
Mastering Emotional Equilibrium

Liberating Emotions: Techniques to Release and Rebalance

Achieving emotional equilibrium is crucial for maintaining mental health and fostering a resilient, balanced life. This chapter focuses on the techniques that help liberate emotions, enabling individuals to release pent-up feelings and rebalance their emotional state. Such practices are not only therapeutic but also enhance one's capacity to engage fully with life's challenges and opportunities.

Understanding Emotional Liberation

Emotional liberation involves recognizing, expressing, and effectively managing emotions so they do not become overwhelming or disruptive. It's about allowing oneself to experience emotions fully, understanding their messages, and then letting them pass without leaving lasting negative impacts.

- Recognition of Emotions: The first step in emotional liberation is to identify and acknowledge emotions as they arise. This involves understanding their triggers and the messages they convey about one's needs and boundaries.
- Expression of Emotions: Safely expressing emotions, whether through art, writing, conversation, or physical activity, helps prevent them from becoming bottled up and potentially harmful.

Techniques for Releasing Emotions

1. Journaling: Writing about feelings and experiences can help process and release emotions. This technique allows for a private, unfiltered exploration of deep-seated feelings.
2. Physical Activity: Engaging in physical exercise is not only good for the body but also for the mind. Activities like running, dancing, or even yoga can help release tension and reduce stress.
3. Artistic Expression: Drawing, painting, or making music provides a conduit for expressing complex emotions, offering a creative and therapeutic outlet for feelings that might be hard to articulate verbally.
4. Guided Imagery and Meditation: These mindfulness practices can help soothe emotional distress and facilitate a deeper understanding of emotional states.

Techniques for Rebalancing Emotions

Once emotions are released, rebalancing them involves restoring emotional harmony through techniques that promote relaxation and positive mood.

1. Deep Breathing Exercises: Techniques such as diaphragmatic breathing help calm the nervous system and reduce the physiological symptoms of stress and anxiety.
2. Mindfulness Meditation: Regular meditation helps maintain an even emotional keel by enhancing present-moment awareness and reducing tendencies toward reactive emotional responses.
3. Positive Reappraisal: Reframing emotional experiences in a more positive or constructive light can shift one's emotional state from negative to positive, aiding in emotional recovery and resilience.
4. Gratitude Practices: Regularly acknowledging things one is grateful for has been shown to improve emotional well-being and life satisfaction.

Implementing Emotional Equilibrium in Daily Life

Integrating these techniques into everyday life ensures that emotional liberation and rebalancing become part of one's routine:

- Routine Check-ins: Regularly scheduled times to check in with oneself emotionally can help maintain awareness of emotional states and needs.
- Setting Emotional Goals: Just like setting career or physical fitness goals, setting emotional goals can provide clear objectives for emotional development and maintenance.
- Seeking Social Support: Engaging with friends, family, or support groups who understand and support one's emotional goals can provide encouragement and accountability.

By mastering the techniques to release and rebalance emotions, individuals equip themselves to handle life's ups and downs more effectively, leading to greater emotional stability and improved overall well-being. This mastery of emotional equilibrium is crucial as individuals advance in their personal development journey, ensuring that they are prepared for complex emotional landscapes and can maintain their mental health and resilience long-term. This foundation is critical as we move into subsequent chapters, where we will explore further strategies for sustaining and building upon this equilibrium to enhance personal and professional life.

Staying Grounded: Managing Triggers and Turmoil

In the journey to master emotional equilibrium, an essential skill is the ability to stay grounded amidst triggers and turmoil. This ability allows individuals to navigate through life's inevitable stresses and emotional upheavals without losing balance. Staying grounded involves techniques that help maintain calmness and clarity during challenging times, ensuring that emotional responses do not escalate into overwhelming states.

Understanding Triggers

A trigger is any stimulus that elicits a strong emotional response. These can be external events, such as conflicts at work or personal relationships, or internal processes, such as memories or thoughts that evoke intense feelings like anxiety or anger.

- Identifying Triggers: The first step in managing triggers is to identify them. Keeping a journal can help track situations, interactions, or thoughts that consistently lead to distress.
- Analyzing Patterns: Once triggers are identified, analyzing the patterns in these responses can provide insights into underlying vulnerabilities or unresolved issues.

Techniques for Staying Grounded

To effectively manage triggers and maintain emotional stability, several grounding techniques can be employed:

1. Mindfulness Practice: Engaging in mindfulness exercises helps anchor oneself in the present moment, reducing the impact of triggering stimuli. Techniques

include focused breathing, sensory grounding (noticing sights, sounds, smells), and mindful walking.

2. Cognitive Reframing: This involves changing the narrative around the trigger to lessen its emotional impact. For example, viewing a stressful event as a challenge rather than a threat can shift one's emotional response from anxiety to motivation.

3. Controlled Breathing Techniques: Slow, deep breathing activates the body's relaxation response, counteracting the surge of adrenaline and cortisol that comes with stress and helping to maintain calm.

4. Physical Grounding Exercises: Physical movements, such as yoga, stretching, or even light exercise, can help release the tension that builds up during stressful situations and bring the focus back to the body.

Building Resilience Against Turmoil

In addition to immediate grounding techniques, building long-term resilience involves creating a lifestyle that supports emotional stability:

- Routine Physical Activity: Regular exercise not only improves physical health but also enhances emotional resilience by reducing symptoms of depression and anxiety.

- Balanced Diet and Sleep: Maintaining a healthy diet and ensuring adequate sleep are crucial for emotional regulation. Sleep deprivation and poor nutrition can exacerbate emotional reactivity.

- Supportive Relationships: Cultivating relationships with people who provide emotional support and understanding can offer a stabilizing influence during times of turmoil.

Implementing a Grounding Routine

Creating a routine that incorporates grounding practices into daily life can prepare one for handling triggers more effectively:

- Daily Mindfulness: Incorporate at least one mindfulness activity into your daily routine, such as morning meditation or evening gratitude reflections.
- Regular Check-ins: Set specific times throughout the day to assess and adjust your emotional state, using brief grounding exercises as needed.
- Emergency Plan: Have a plan for intense situations, including a list of activities, contacts, and thoughts that can help recenter and destress quickly.

Staying grounded is not just about managing moments of crisis but also about cultivating a steady base from which to approach life's challenges. By mastering these techniques, individuals enhance their ability to navigate through emotional triggers and turmoil effectively, ensuring that their path towards emotional equilibrium is maintained. This preparation is vital as they continue to explore deeper aspects of personal development, ensuring that they are equipped to handle whatever challenges may arise.

Building Emotional Agility: Strategies for Responsive Living

Emotional agility is the skill to navigate life's twists and turns with flexibility, awareness, and acceptance. By developing emotional agility, individuals can respond to varying situations with a balanced and thoughtful approach rather than reacting based on entrenched habits or emotional impulses. This section explores strategies to enhance emotional agility, facilitating a more responsive and adaptive approach to both personal challenges and opportunities.

Understanding Emotional Agility

Emotional agility involves being able to manage one's thoughts and feelings in a way that is conscious, deliberate, and aligned with one's values. It means moving away from automatic emotional reactions and towards choices that sustain growth and well-being.

- Self-Awareness: The foundation of emotional agility is a deep understanding of one's emotions, triggers, and the habitual responses that might not always serve well.
- Acceptance: This involves accepting emotions without judgment. Acknowledging feelings without labelling them as 'good' or 'bad' allows for a more objective and calm assessment of what they signify.

Strategies for Enhancing Emotional Agility

Developing emotional agility requires consistent practice and integration of various strategies into daily life:

1. Cognitive Flexibility: Learning to think about situations in multiple ways can help prevent getting stuck in negative thought patterns. Techniques such as reframing or looking at a situation from different perspectives are crucial.
2. Emotional Decompression: Giving oneself time and space to process emotions before responding. This might mean taking a few deep breaths during a stressful moment or allowing some time to pass before addressing a conflict.
3. Regular Reflection: Engaging in regular reflection enhances emotional understanding and agility. This could be through meditation, journaling, or therapy sessions where thoughts and emotions are explored and dissected.

4. Value Alignment: Making decisions based on personal values rather than immediate emotional impulses. This requires clear understanding and articulation of what truly matters in one's life.

Practical Application of Emotional Agility

Implementing emotional agility in everyday situations enhances one's ability to live responsively:

- Active Listening: Listening to others without immediately reacting or forming a response in your head allows for more thoughtful and understanding interactions.
- Mindful Communication: Communicating in a way that is reflective, considering the emotional content of the conversation and responding accordingly.
- Flexible Problem-Solving: Approaching problems with an open mind, ready to adapt strategies as new information and perspectives arise.

Sustaining Emotional Agility

To sustain emotional agility over the long term, it is important to:

- Continuous Learning: Engage in lifelong learning about emotional health and psychological growth. Stay updated with new insights from psychology and neuroscience that can inform personal practices.
- Community Engagement: Participate in groups or workshops that focus on developing emotional skills. Learning from and with others can provide new tools and support.
- Regular Practice: Like any other skill, emotional agility improves with regular practice. Incorporate agility exercises into daily routines to make them second nature.

Building and maintaining emotional agility prepares individuals for a life of adaptive and fulfilling interactions, both with themselves and others. It lays the groundwork for the next chapter in their development journey, which focuses on integrating these skills into broader life contexts. In the next chapter, we will explore how these cultivated skills of emotional equilibrium and agility enhance not just personal well-being but also professional and social interactions, ensuring that individuals are equipped to handle diverse and complex life scenarios with grace and effectiveness.

Chapter 11 Summary

Chapter 11, "Mastering Emotional Equilibrium," emphasizes techniques for achieving emotional stability by learning to effectively manage and balance emotions. The chapter introduces methods to recognize, express, and regulate emotions to prevent them from becoming overwhelming. Key techniques include journaling, physical activity, artistic expression, and guided imagery for releasing emotions, alongside deep breathing exercises and mindfulness meditation for rebalancing emotional states.

To implement these techniques into daily routines, the chapter suggests regular emotional check-ins, setting specific emotional goals, and seeking social support to reinforce emotional management strategies. By mastering these practices, individuals can handle life's challenges with greater resilience, maintaining mental health and overall well-being. The skills acquired also prepare individuals for advanced personal development, ensuring they can maintain emotional stability in complex scenarios.

MY NOTES

Architecting Secure Relationships with CBT

Foundations of Trust and Mutual Respect Through Behavioral Change

Creating secure relationships is essential for emotional well-being and life satisfaction. Cognitive-Behavioral Therapy (CBT) offers valuable strategies for building and maintaining trust and mutual respect through intentional behavioral changes. This chapter outlines how CBT techniques can be directly applied to enhance relational dynamics, fostering environments of trust and respect that are critical for healthy relationships.

Leveraging CBT for Relationship Enhancement

CBT is a practical framework that helps individuals modify unhelpful cognitive and behavioral patterns. In the context of relationships, CBT focuses on enhancing communication, managing emotions, and changing behaviors that undermine trust and respect.

- Cognitive Restructuring: This involves identifying and challenging negative thoughts about oneself or one's partner that can damage relationships. By reframing these thoughts, individuals can reduce misunderstandings and increase empathy.

- Behavioral Adjustments: CBT encourages the adoption of positive behaviors that reinforce trust and respect, such as reliability, openness, and proactive conflict resolution.

Strategies to Build Trust with CBT

Trust is the cornerstone of any strong relationship. Here are some CBT strategies specifically tailored to enhance trust:

1. Consistency and Predictability: Use CBT to develop and maintain consistent behaviors. Reliability in small actions builds a foundation of trust over time.
2. Transparency in Communication: Practice open communication about thoughts, feelings, and intentions. CBT techniques like assertiveness training can help individuals express themselves clearly and respectfully, reducing the chances of misunderstandings.
3. Problem-Solving Skills: Employ CBT strategies to improve joint problem-solving capabilities, ensuring that both partners feel heard and valued during conflicts or decisions, which enhances trust.

Promoting Mutual Respect with CBT

Mutual respect is equally important and can be cultivated through these CBT techniques:

1. Empathic Listening: Train in active listening skills to fully understand and appreciate your partner's perspective. This not only validates their feelings but also promotes a respectful interaction environment.

2. Respecting Boundaries: Use CBT to identify and respect personal and relational boundaries. Exercises in boundary-setting can be beneficial for both partners to feel safe and valued.

3. Handling Criticism Constructively: Learn and apply CBT methods to give and receive feedback in ways that are constructive rather than destructive, fostering an atmosphere of mutual respect.

Practical Implementation of CBT in Relationships

To effectively integrate CBT into daily relational interactions, consider the following practical applications:

- Regular Practice: Engage in daily or weekly practices that reinforce CBT skills. This could include scheduled discussions where partners share their feelings and work on communication strategies.
- CBT Sessions for Couples: Participating in CBT sessions with a qualified therapist can provide a guided framework for addressing specific relationship issues and developing healthy coping strategies.
- Self-Help Resources: Utilize CBT-based self-help books or online resources to continue learning and practicing skills independently or together with a partner.

By systematically applying these CBT strategies, individuals and couples can build stronger foundations of trust and mutual respect, essential for the long-term success of any relationship. This approach not only helps in resolving existing issues but also equips partners with the tools to effectively manage future challenges, ensuring a dynamic and resilient relationship.

As relationships evolve and partners continue to grow both individually and together, maintaining these CBT practices is crucial for sustaining the improvements achieved. In subsequent chapters, we will explore further techniques to continue enhancing relationship quality, focusing on advanced strategies for maintaining and renewing commitment and connection over time. This continuous improvement approach ensures that relationships not only endure but thrive in the face of life's inevitable changes and stresses.

Balancing Independence with Interdependence: CBT *Interventions*

Achieving a balance between independence and interdependence is crucial for healthy, fulfilling relationships. Cognitive-Behavioral Therapy (CBT) offers practical interventions to help individuals and couples navigate this balance effectively. This section delves into CBT strategies designed to foster both personal autonomy and a collaborative partnership, enhancing the overall quality and durability of relationships.

Understanding the Dynamics of Independence and Interdependence

Independence in a relationship refers to the ability of each person to maintain their sense of self and engage in activities outside of the relationship without excessive reliance on their partner. Interdependence, on the other hand, involves a mutual dependence where both partners benefit from and contribute to the relationship in a way that respects individual autonomy.

- Identifying Imbalances: CBT can help identify whether a relationship leans too heavily towards independence (resulting in disconnection) or interdependence (leading to enmeshment). Recognizing these imbalances is the first step toward addressing them.

CBT Interventions for Enhancing Independence

Promoting healthy independence within a relationship involves encouraging each partner to pursue their personal interests and responsibilities, which fosters self-esteem and reduces resentment.

1. Self-Reflection Exercises: Use CBT techniques to explore personal values, interests, and goals independent of the relationship. This can help clarify what aspects of independence are most important to each partner.
2. Boundary Setting: CBT can assist in clearly defining and communicating personal boundaries to a partner. This includes discussing how much space, time, and freedom each person needs to feel fulfilled independently.
3. Assertiveness Training: Develop assertiveness skills through CBT to express needs and desires without fear of conflict or guilt. This helps ensure that independence does not morph into isolation.

CBT Interventions for Fostering Interdependence

Interdependence is strengthened when partners can rely on each other in ways that are supportive and do not compromise individual autonomy.

1. Communication Skills Development: Enhance communication strategies through CBT to discuss needs, expectations, and how to support each other effectively. This includes learning to ask for help when needed and offering support without overstepping boundaries.
2. Joint Problem-Solving: Implement CBT techniques to improve collaborative problem-solving, ensuring that both partners contribute to decisions and solutions. This promotes a sense of teamwork and shared responsibility.
3. Empathy Enhancement: Use CBT exercises to increase empathy within the relationship, helping partners understand and appreciate each other's unique perspectives and emotional experiences.

Implementing Balanced Dynamics in Daily Life

Incorporating these CBT interventions into daily life requires consistent practice and commitment from both partners:

- Regular Relationship Check-Ins: Schedule regular discussions to assess how well the balance between independence and interdependence is being maintained. Adjust as necessary based on these conversations.
- Couple Activities: Plan activities that require teamwork and cooperation, reinforcing interdependence. Simultaneously, encourage time apart for individual activities to maintain independence.
- Therapy Sessions: Consider couples therapy with a CBT focus to address specific issues related to balancing independence and interdependence. A therapist can provide personalized strategies and guidance.

Balancing independence with interdependence using CBT interventions creates a relationship dynamic that supports personal growth while strengthening the bond between partners. This balance is essential for the relationship's health and longevity, ensuring that each partner feels valued and supported both as an individual and as part of a couple. As we move forward, these principles can be continuously refined and adapted to meet the evolving needs of each partner and the relationship as a whole, fostering a sustainable and fulfilling partnership.

Drafting a Blueprint for Lasting Bonds with Cognitive Techniques

In any successful relationship, having a well-thought-out blueprint that outlines the fundamental aspects of building and maintaining lasting bonds is crucial. Cognitive techniques, particularly those derived from Cognitive-Behavioral Therapy (CBT), provide effective tools for crafting such a blueprint. These techniques help individuals and couples develop a clear plan for nurturing relationships that are not only fulfilling but also resilient over time.

Foundations of a Relationship Blueprint

The blueprint for a lasting relationship focuses on establishing strong communication, mutual understanding, and shared goals, all of which are reinforced by cognitive techniques.

- Setting Relationship Goals: Use cognitive techniques to help both partners articulate and align their relationship goals. This may involve exercises to clarify individual expectations and find common ground.
- Developing Communication Strategies: Cognitive techniques can be employed to enhance communication skills, teaching partners how to express their thoughts and feelings clearly and constructively without misinterpretations or assumptions.
- Fostering Emotional Intelligence: Training in cognitive methods can enhance emotional intelligence by helping individuals recognize their own and their partner's emotional patterns, fostering greater empathy and responsiveness.

Cognitive Techniques for Relationship Maintenance

To ensure the longevity of relationships, cognitive techniques can be applied to continuously manage and resolve conflicts, deepen intimacy, and adapt to life changes.

1. Cognitive Restructuring: This involves identifying and modifying any negative thought patterns that may lead to misunderstandings or conflicts. By reframing how situations are perceived, partners can respond to each other more positively and compassionately.

2. Problem-Solving Techniques: Equip couples with cognitive strategies for effective problem-solving, emphasizing rational analysis and cooperative solutions that satisfy both partners' needs.

3. Preventative Maintenance: Implement cognitive routines that help anticipate and address potential relationship issues before they become problematic. This includes regular assessments of the relationship's health and proactive communication.

Integrating Cognitive Techniques into Daily Routines

To make these cognitive techniques effective, they should be integrated into the couple's daily routines and interactions:

- Daily Cognitive Exercises: Encourage partners to engage in daily exercises such as gratitude lists or positive affirmations about each other to strengthen emotional connections and positive perceptions.

- Routine Check-Ins: Establish a routine of regular check-ins where partners can discuss their relationship status, celebrate achievements, and address concerns using cognitive approaches.

- Adaptation and Flexibility: Teach partners to use cognitive flexibility to adapt to changes in the relationship or external circumstances, ensuring that the relationship can evolve without losing its core values and objectives.

Building Towards Future Growth

The application of cognitive techniques in crafting and maintaining a relationship blueprint lays a solid foundation for current and future happiness and stability. This proactive approach ensures that partners not only resolve current issues but also develop the skills and attitudes necessary for long-term success and mutual satisfaction.

As we progress to the next chapter, we will explore how these foundational strategies translate into practical applications in everyday life, particularly focusing on intimacy and practical engagement in relationships. Chapter 13 will delve into the application of these cognitive techniques in real-life scenarios, enhancing day-to-day interactions and ensuring that partners continue to grow together harmoniously.

Chapter 12 Summary

Chapter 12, "Architecting Secure Relationships with CBT," explores how Cognitive-Behavioral Therapy (CBT) can be applied to strengthen relational dynamics, fostering trust and mutual respect, which are foundational for secure relationships. The chapter details techniques such as cognitive restructuring to challenge negative thoughts, and behavioral adjustments to enhance communication and conflict resolution.

It presents strategies to build trust, emphasizing consistency, transparency, and effective problem-solving, while promoting mutual respect through empathic listening, respecting boundaries, and constructive feedback. Practical implementation includes regular CBT practices, couples therapy sessions, and utilizing self-help resources to reinforce relationship skills.

Furthermore, the chapter discusses balancing independence with interdependence using CBT, helping couples manage personal space while fostering a supportive partnership. Techniques include setting personal boundaries, enhancing communication, and developing joint problem-solving skills.

Overall, the chapter provides a blueprint for using cognitive techniques to establish and maintain lasting bonds, emphasizing routine practice, and adapting strategies to ensure relational stability and satisfaction.

MY NOTES

Chapter 13

Intimacy in Action

Fostering Intimacy: Practical CBT Approaches for Everyday Connection

Intimacy is a crucial component of any thriving relationship, encompassing emotional, intellectual, and sometimes physical closeness between partners. Cognitive-Behavioral Therapy (CBT) offers practical approaches that can help couples enhance intimacy by improving communication, increasing emotional understanding, and resolving conflicts effectively. This chapter explores how to apply CBT techniques to deepen intimacy in everyday interactions, enhancing the connection and strength of the relationship.

Enhancing Communication Skills

Effective communication is the backbone of intimacy. CBT provides tools to improve how partners communicate, ensuring that both individuals feel heard, understood, and valued.

- Active Listening Techniques: Teach partners to practice active listening, which involves fully concentrating on what is being said rather than passively hearing the message of the speaker. This includes nonverbal cues such as nodding, maintaining eye contact, and verbal affirmations like "I understand" or "Tell me more."

- Expressive Communication Training: Use CBT to help individuals express their thoughts and feelings clearly and respectfully. This might involve role-playing exercises to practice expressing emotions in a way that is constructive rather than accusatory.
- Conflict Resolution Skills: Equip partners with strategies to handle disagreements in a way that promotes understanding rather than discord. Techniques include identifying automatic negative thoughts that can escalate conflicts and learning to replace them with more rational, calm responses.

Building Emotional Connection

Intimacy is deeply rooted in emotional connection. CBT strategies can be used to build and enhance this connection by helping partners understand and respond to each other's emotional needs.

- Emotion Identification Exercises: Encourage partners to practice identifying and discussing their emotions. This can be facilitated through 'emotion logs' or 'emotion sharing' sessions where each person describes how they felt during specific incidents and why.
- Empathy Development: Implement exercises that boost empathy, such as imagining oneself in the partner's situation or discussing how each partner might have felt during certain events.
- Enhancing Emotional Responsiveness: Teach partners to respond to each other's emotional expressions in ways that validate and support each other, rather than minimizing or dismissing feelings.

Creating Opportunities for Connection

Intimacy doesn't just happen; it needs to be cultivated actively. CBT provides a framework for creating and taking advantage of opportunities to connect.

- Regular Date Nights: Schedule regular times dedicated solely to the relationship. Use CBT techniques to plan activities that both partners enjoy and that encourage interaction and connection.
- Intimacy Rituals: Develop small daily or weekly rituals that foster intimacy, such as having coffee together every morning, sharing a hug before leaving for work, or a nightly check-in conversation.
- Gratitude Practices: Integrate practices that focus on showing appreciation for each other, such as verbally expressing gratitude for one's partner or writing appreciation notes.

Integrating CBT into Daily Life

To make these CBT strategies part of everyday life, consistency is key.

- Daily Practice: Encourage couples to integrate at least one CBT technique into their daily routine, such as a brief couple's meditation or a gratitude sharing moment.
- CBT Sessions: Regular sessions with a CBT therapist can help reinforce these practices, provide new insights, and adjust strategies as the relationship evolves.
- Self-Guided Activities: Provide couples with resources such as books, apps, or worksheets that offer guided activities based on CBT principles.

By integrating these practical CBT approaches into their daily interactions, couples can significantly enhance the intimacy and strength of their relationship. These techniques not only help resolve current issues but also lay the groundwork for a continually evolving and deepening connection. As couples become proficient in these practices, they establish a durable framework for intimacy that supports a fulfilling and enduring relationship. This ongoing cultivation of intimacy sets the stage for the next chapter, which explores sustaining and nurturing these connections over the long term, ensuring that relationships not only survive but thrive.

The Chemistry of Attachment: Navigating Compatibility and Connection

Understanding the chemistry of attachment is essential for fostering deep and enduring connections in relationships. This segment explores the interplay between psychological theories of attachment and practical approaches to enhancing compatibility and connection between partners. By integrating insights from attachment theory with cognitive-behavioral strategies, couples can better navigate the complexities of their relationships and enhance their emotional bonds.

Understanding Attachment Styles

Attachment theory provides a framework for understanding how people relate to others in intimate relationships based on their early experiences with caregivers. Recognizing and understanding one's attachment style—be it secure, anxious, avoidant, or fearful-avoidant—can provide significant insights into how one forms and maintains relationships.

- Identifying Attachment Styles: Use assessments and reflections to help partners identify their own and each other's attachment styles. This understanding can foster greater empathy and patience in navigating relationship dynamics.
- Discussing the Impact: Facilitate discussions about how these styles influence individual behaviors and relationship interactions, including needs for independence, closeness, and emotional response patterns.

Enhancing Compatibility with CBT

Cognitive-Behavioral Therapy (CBT) offers tools that can help partners understand and adapt to each other's attachment needs, enhancing compatibility.

- Reframing Thoughts: Teach partners to reframe thoughts that arise from insecure attachment tendencies, such as fear of abandonment or discomfort with closeness, into more constructive perspectives that promote understanding and connection.
- Behavioral Adjustments: Encourage behaviors that foster security within the relationship, such as consistently responding to each other's bids for attention, communicating openly about needs and expectations, and reliably being there for each other.

Building Connection Through Emotional Attunement

Deepening connection in a relationship involves aligning with each other's emotional states through attunement—a process where partners respond to each other's emotional needs and signals effectively.

- Practicing Active Listening: Use CBT techniques to enhance active listening skills, where partners not only hear but truly understand and empathize with each other's feelings and perspectives.
- Expressing Validation: Guide partners in expressing validation and acknowledgment of each other's emotions, which can help strengthen the emotional bond and build a secure base in the relationship.
- Conflict Resolution: Equip couples with strategies to manage conflicts in ways that respect each partner's attachment needs, ensuring that disagreements strengthen rather than weaken the relationship bond.

Practical Exercises for Enhancing Attachment

To help couples apply these concepts in their daily lives, practical exercises can be integrated into their routine:

- Attachment Style Workshops: Participate in workshops or therapy sessions focused on exploring and addressing attachment styles, where couples can learn more about each other and how to support each other's growth.
- Daily Connection Rituals: Establish daily rituals that reinforce connection, such as sharing a moment of gratitude, engaging in a few minutes of uninterrupted conversation, or practicing a nightly routine that includes time to reconnect physically and emotionally.
- Regular Relationship Check-Ins: Schedule regular check-ins to discuss the relationship's health, areas for improvement, and celebrate successes in navigating attachment-related challenges.

By understanding and addressing the chemistry of attachment, couples can create a more harmonious and fulfilling relationship. The strategies discussed not only help mitigate the challenges associated with differing attachment styles but also promote a deeper sense of compatibility and connection. This foundational work in attachment and connection is vital as it prepares couples for the ongoing journey of relationship growth, setting the stage for the next chapter, which will explore sustaining and nurturing these connections over the long term, ensuring that relationships continue to thrive and adapt through life's various phases.

The 'We' in Wellness: Co-Creating Relationship Health Through Behavioral Activation

In nurturing a healthy relationship, both partners must actively participate in creating and maintaining wellness. Behavioral activation, a strategy derived from Cognitive-Behavioral Therapy (CBT), offers a structured approach to enhancing relationship health by encouraging activities that promote positive interactions and mutual satisfaction. This section discusses how couples can use behavioral activation to strengthen their partnership, enhancing overall wellness together.

Understanding Behavioral Activation

Behavioral activation focuses on increasing engagement in positive and meaningful activities to improve mood and alter behavior. In the context of a relationship, this means jointly participating in activities that both partners find enjoyable and fulfilling, which can lead to improved relationship satisfaction and emotional health.

- Identifying Shared Interests: Begin by identifying activities that both partners enjoy or have expressed interest in trying together. This could range from outdoor activities, cooking together, cultural outings, or participating in shared hobbies.

- Scheduling Regular Activities: Make a commitment to regularly schedule these activities. Consistency plays a key role in behavioral activation, reinforcing positive experiences and interactions that strengthen the relationship.

Enhancing Emotional Connection Through Shared Activities

Shared activities not only provide enjoyment but also serve as opportunities for partners to connect on deeper emotional levels, facilitating communication and understanding.

- Quality Time Together: Use these activities as a guaranteed time for quality interaction, free from the distractions of daily life and responsibilities.
- Building New Experiences: Continuously incorporate new activities to keep the relationship dynamic and interesting. This helps prevent routines from becoming stale and encourages ongoing engagement and excitement.
- Reinforcing Positive Interaction: Focus on the positive aspects of each activity, using them as opportunities to show appreciation, offer support, and build a stronger emotional bond.

Practical Tips for Implementing Behavioral Activation

To effectively implement behavioral activation in a relationship, consider the following practical tips:

- Mutual Planning: Involve both partners in the planning process to ensure that activities meet both partners' interests and needs. This participation fosters a sense of teamwork and mutual investment in the relationship's health.

- Goal Setting: Set specific, achievable goals for what each partner hopes to gain from these activities, whether it's improving health, learning a new skill, or simply spending more time together.
- Feedback and Adaptation: After engaging in activities, discuss what went well and what could be improved. This feedback loop is essential for adapting activities to better suit the relationship's evolving needs.

Integrating Wellness into Everyday Life

Integrating these strategies requires deliberate effort and regular practice:

- Daily Wellness Checks: Incorporate brief daily check-ins where each partner can express how they feel about the relationship and any ideas for new activities or adjustments to current practices.
- Celebrating Achievements: Regularly acknowledge and celebrate the successes and efforts made in enhancing the relationship's wellness, reinforcing the value of continued effort and participation.

By actively participating in behavioral activation strategies, couples can significantly enhance their relationship health, creating a robust 'we' in wellness. This proactive approach not only improves the current state of the relationship but also sets a strong foundation for future growth and deeper connection.

As this chapter concludes, the preparation for the next chapter, Chapter 14: Guide for Partners and Loved Ones, becomes evident. Here, we will explore how to extend these behavioral activation strategies to include broader family dynamics and support systems, enhancing relationship health not just between partners but across the entire network of loved ones. This expansion ensures that the benefits of relationship wellness are amplified and shared, contributing to a supportive and nurturing community environment.

Chapter 13 Summary

Chapter 13, "Intimacy in Action," explores practical Cognitive-Behavioral Therapy (CBT) strategies to enhance intimacy in relationships through improved communication, emotional understanding, and conflict resolution.

The chapter highlights how to deepen connections daily by focusing on effective communication techniques, including active listening and expressive communication training, which ensure both partners feel heard and understood.

It details building emotional connections by identifying emotions, developing empathy, and responding supportively to enhance emotional intimacy. Practical suggestions for fostering intimacy include scheduling regular date nights, establishing daily rituals, and expressing gratitude, all aimed at strengthening the relational bond.

The chapter emphasizes integrating CBT into daily interactions through consistent practice, regular CBT sessions, and self-guided activities to maintain and enhance the relationship's intimacy. By applying these CBT techniques, couples can improve their communication, deepen their emotional connection, and actively cultivate a fulfilling and resilient relationship.

MY NOTES

Guide for Partners and Loved Ones

Understanding the Avoidant Heart: A Companion's Guide

Developing a meaningful relationship with someone who has an avoidant attachment style can be complex. This chapter serves as a practical guide for partners and loved ones on how to better understand and effectively connect with individuals displaying avoidant behaviors. By applying empathetic insights and supportive strategies, relationships can grow stronger and more fulfilling, even in the face of emotional distancing.

Key Characteristics of Avoidant Attachment

Avoidant attachment often manifests as a need for independence and self-sufficiency, with a marked discomfort with closeness and emotional expression. Understanding these characteristics is crucial:

- Emotional Distance: Avoidant individuals may seem aloof or emotionally distant, especially in situations that demand closeness.
- Self-Reliance: A strong preference for handling issues alone without seeking help or sharing burdens.
- Commitment Wary: Hesitancy or reluctance to commit fully to relationships, often due to a deep-rooted fear of dependency.

Strategies for Building Connection

Building a connection with an avoidant partner requires patience, understanding, and specific strategies that respect their need for space while gradually promoting intimacy.

1. Give Space Generously: Recognize and respect the need for independence. Pushing too hard for closeness can lead to withdrawal, so it's important to let the avoidant partner set the pace for intimacy.
2. Promote Open Communication: Establish an environment where open and non-judgmental communication is encouraged. Ensure that conversations about needs and expectations are clear but not demanding.
3. Support Without Smothering: Offer support and assistance but allow your avoidant partner the freedom to accept help on their terms. This balance helps build trust without triggering avoidance.

Enhancing Emotional Understanding

Fostering a deeper emotional connection involves understanding the underlying fears and behaviors associated with avoidant attachment.

- Educate Yourself: Learn about avoidant attachment through books, articles, or counseling to better understand the motivations and fears that drive your partner's behaviors.
- Encourage Gradual Change: Support your partner in taking small steps towards greater openness and vulnerability. Celebrate these moments of courage and connection.
- Practice Patience: Change takes time, especially in fundamental aspects of personality like attachment styles. Continuous patience and understanding are vital.

Practical Tools for Partners and Loved Ones

To effectively support an avoidant partner, incorporating practical tools can be helpful:

- Couple's Therapy: Engaging in couple's therapy with a focus on attachment can provide structured support and guidance for navigating avoidant tendencies.
- Behavioral Techniques: Utilize techniques from Cognitive Behavioral Therapy (CBT) to help manage reactions to avoidant behaviors and to encourage positive interactions.
- Regular Check-ins: Establish a routine that includes regular, non-invasive check-ins that allow for the sharing of thoughts and feelings in a safe space.

Understanding and adapting to the needs of someone with an avoidant attachment style is challenging but deeply rewarding. This guide provides a foundation for partners and loved ones to foster greater intimacy and stronger bonds by respecting boundaries, encouraging open communication, and practicing patience and understanding.

Compassionate Coping: When They Withdraw

Navigating moments when a partner with an avoidant attachment style withdraws can be challenging. Understanding how to respond compassionately and effectively is essential for maintaining a healthy relationship dynamic. This section provides practical strategies for managing these periods, ensuring both partners feel supported and understood.

Understanding Withdrawal in Avoidant Attachment

Withdrawal is a typical behavior for individuals with avoidant attachment when they feel overwhelmed or perceive a threat to their independence. Recognizing and understanding this pattern is the first step:

- Identify Triggers: Observe and note the situations or emotional states that trigger withdrawal. These might include conflicts, discussions about the future, or emotional demands.
- Acknowledge the Need for Space: Understand that withdrawal is often a self-protective mechanism, not a rejection or lack of affection.

Strategies for Compassionate Coping

Effective coping strategies can help maintain connection and respect each partner's needs during periods of withdrawal:

1. Maintain Emotional Equilibrium: Manage your own emotions to prevent escalating the situation. Practicing mindfulness and self-soothing techniques can help you remain composed.
2. Give Space Graciously: Allow your partner the necessary space without feeling neglected or resentful. Communicate that you are available when they are ready to reconnect, but do not pressure them to engage before they are prepared.
3. Use Non-Confrontational Communication: When it's time to discuss the issue, use "I" statements to express how the withdrawal impacts you, rather than assigning blame or criticism. For example, say, "I feel a bit disconnected when we don't talk about our feelings," rather than, "You always shut me out."

Building a Foundation for Reconnection

Facilitating a positive reconnection after a period of withdrawal is crucial for strengthening the relationship:

- Initiate Low-Pressure Interaction: Engage in activities that are undemanding and relaxing, like watching a favorite show together or taking a walk.
- Express Appreciation and Affection: When your partner begins to re-engage, show appreciation for their presence and efforts. Small gestures of affection can reinforce their decision to reconnect.
- Encourage Open Discussion About Needs: Once tensions have eased, discuss what each of you needs during these withdrawal periods to better understand each other without judgment or pressure.

Promoting Understanding and Growth

Continual effort to understand each other's needs and responses is vital for relationship growth:

- Reflect on Each Incident: After a withdrawal episode, reflect on what triggered it and how both of you handled the situation. Consider what might be done differently next time to manage it more effectively.
- Develop Joint Strategies: Together, develop strategies that cater to both the need for space and the desire for closeness. This could include agreeing on a signal that your partner can use when they need space, so it's not taken personally.
- Reaffirm Commitment Regularly: Regularly reassure each other of your commitment to the relationship and to working through attachment-related challenges together.

By adopting these compassionate coping strategies, partners can better manage the moments of withdrawal that come with an avoidant attachment style, leading to a more understanding and supportive relationship. This approach not only assists in navigating immediate challenges but also paves the way for deeper intimacy and stronger bonds.

Together Through the Maze: Support Strategies for Mixed Attachment Styles

Navigating relationships where partners have different attachment styles can be like moving through a maze, with each turn presenting new challenges and opportunities for growth. This section explores effective support strategies that help partners with mixed attachment styles understand each other better and strengthen their relationship.

Recognizing the Impact of Mixed Attachment Styles

Understanding the dynamics of mixed attachment styles—such as secure with avoidant, anxious with secure, or any other combination—is critical for managing interactions and expectations. Each style brings its unique perspective on closeness, communication, and conflict, influencing the relationship's overall dynamic.

- Identify Each Partner's Style: Clearly identifying and acknowledging each partner's attachment style helps predict potential conflicts and misunderstandings, setting the stage for more effective communication and problem-solving.
- Educate About Differences: Learning about how different attachment styles affect perceptions and behaviors can foster empathy and patience, crucial for navigating the complexities of mixed attachment styles.

Strategies for Support and Enhancement

Adapting to and supporting each other in a relationship with mixed attachment styles requires specific strategies that cater to the needs and comfort levels of both partners.

1. Developing Communication Skills: Tailor communication strategies to fit the attachment styles of both partners. For instance, someone with an avoidant style may prefer more space and less emotional intensity, while someone with an anxious style might need more reassurance and frequent contact.
2. Balancing Needs for Closeness and Independence: Find a balance that respects the avoidant partner's need for independence and the anxious partner's need for closeness. This might involve negotiating specific times for togetherness and alone time.
3. Conflict Resolution Techniques: Utilize conflict resolution strategies that consider the sensitivities of each attachment style. For example, approaching conflicts with calm, structured conversations can help an anxious partner feel secure and an avoidant partner feel less overwhelmed.

Practical Exercises for Mixed Attachment Styles

Implementing practical exercises can help couples with mixed attachment styles strengthen their relationship:

- Attachment Style Workshops: Participate in workshops or therapy sessions designed to help couples understand and adapt to their mixed attachment styles.
- Regular Relationship Check-Ins: Establish a routine for regular check-ins that allow both partners to voice their feelings and concerns in a safe and supportive environment.

- Couples Activities Designed for Bonding: Engage in planned activities that encourage bonding and understanding, such as couples retreats, team-building exercises, or joint hobbies that suit both partners' interests.

Understanding and navigating the complexities of mixed attachment styles require patience, dedication, and continuous effort from both partners. By implementing the strategies outlined above, couples can enhance their ability to support each other through the challenges and enjoy a deeper, more fulfilling relationship.

These principles and techniques for navigating mixed attachment styles pave the way for the discussions in Chapter 15: Synergizing Attachment Styles. This upcoming chapter will delve deeper into how couples can effectively harmonize their differing attachment tendencies to enhance mutual understanding, cooperation, and emotional connection in their relationships.

Chapter 14 Summary

Chapter 14, "Guide for Partners and Loved Ones," provides a comprehensive approach for individuals involved with partners who exhibit avoidant attachment styles. The chapter emphasizes understanding the characteristics of avoidant attachment, such as a preference for independence, emotional distance, and reluctance to commit. It suggests strategies for building a connection that respects the partner's need for space while encouraging closer emotional ties.

Key strategies include allowing space generously, promoting open communication, and supporting without smothering, which help in gradually building trust and intimacy. The chapter also advocates for enhancing emotional understanding through education about avoidant attachment, encouraging small steps toward openness, and practicing patience.

Additionally, it includes practical tools like couple's therapy, behavioral techniques, and regular non-invasive check-ins to facilitate this understanding and adaptation.

By implementing these approaches, partners and loved ones can develop stronger, more understanding relationships with those who have avoidant attachment styles, fostering greater intimacy and a supportive partnership environment.

MY NOTES

Chapter 15

Synergizing Attachment Styles

The Convergence: When Opposite Attachments Attract

When individuals with different attachment styles form relationships, they face unique challenges, but they also have unique opportunities to grow and enrich each other's emotional lives. This chapter explores how partners with divergent attachment styles—such as secure with anxious, avoidant with secure, or any other combination—can synergize their differences to create a balanced, harmonious relationship.

Understanding the Dynamics of Opposite Attachment Styles

Divergent attachment styles can lead to misunderstandings and conflicts, but they also offer a platform for profound personal growth and mutual understanding. Recognizing and appreciating the strengths and vulnerabilities that each style brings to the relationship is the first step in creating synergy.

- Identifying Complementary Qualities: Each attachment style has qualities that can complement the other. For example, the stability and warmth of a secure partner can help soothe the anxiety of an anxious partner, while the independence of an avoidant partner can help a secure partner explore their own autonomy.

- Educating Each Other on Personal Triggers: Partners should communicate openly about their sensitivities and triggers. This mutual understanding helps prevent conflicts and strengthens the bond.

Strategies for Creating Synergy

Creating a synergistic relationship involves intentional strategies designed to accommodate and leverage the strengths of each partner's attachment style.

1. Balancing Needs: Develop a plan that respects the need for closeness of one partner and the need for space of the other. This might involve setting clear boundaries and expectations that both partners agree upon.
2. Emotional Regulation Techniques: Teach and practice emotional regulation techniques together. For instance, partners can use deep breathing, mindfulness, or positive reframing to manage emotional reactions before they escalate into conflict.
3. Enhancing Communication: Foster an environment where open, honest communication is encouraged. Use structured communication techniques like scheduled talks, where each partner can express their thoughts and feelings without interruption.

Practical Exercises for Synergizing Attachment Styles

To actively work on synergizing attachment styles, couples can engage in specific exercises that promote understanding and adjustment:

- Role Reversal Exercises: Temporarily adopting each other's roles can help partners understand the emotional landscape of the other. This exercise promotes empathy and insight into each other's behaviors and needs.

- Joint Journaling: Keeping a relationship journal where both partners can express their daily feelings and thoughts about the relationship can enhance understanding and provide insights into how to better support each other.
- Attachment Style Playbooks: Create a "playbook" for each partner that includes tips, strategies, and approaches that have been effective in addressing their attachment needs. This resource can be referred to in times of stress or misunderstanding.

Synergizing divergent attachment styles requires dedication, patience, and a willingness to grow both individually and as a couple. By understanding each other's attachment styles and actively working to harmonize their interactions, partners can transform their differences into strengths, leading to a more satisfying and resilient relationship.

These strategies not only help couples in the present but also prepare them for future challenges, ensuring that their relationship continues to evolve and deepen. As partners learn to effectively synergize their attachment styles, they build a strong foundation that supports both individual satisfaction and collective harmony. This solid foundation enhances the relationship's ability to adapt and flourish, making it a continuous source of support and happiness for both partners.

Cultivating a Mutual Path to Secure Attachment

In relationships where partners have different attachment styles, finding a mutual path to secure attachment is a pivotal goal. This process involves adopting behaviors and communication strategies that promote security, trust, and understanding for both individuals. By fostering a more secure attachment style within the relationship, couples can experience deeper intimacy, improved conflict resolution, and enhanced overall relationship satisfaction.

Principles of Secure Attachment

Secure attachment in relationships is characterized by trust, a balance of independence and interdependence, and the ability to manage emotions and conflicts effectively. Cultivating this within a relationship where one or both partners initially have insecure attachment styles involves several key principles:

- Consistency and Reliability: Regular, predictable behaviors such as consistently being emotionally available and following through on commitments help build trust and security.
- Open and Honest Communication: Encouraging an environment where both partners feel safe to express their thoughts, feelings, and needs without fear of judgment or retaliation.
- Validating Each Other's Feelings: Acknowledge and respect each other's emotions without necessarily trying to change them. This validation helps both partners feel understood and supported.

Strategies to Foster Secure Attachment

Implementing specific strategies can help partners move toward a more secure attachment style, enhancing the relationship's health and longevity.

1. Creating a Safe Emotional Space: Develop practices that ensure both partners feel emotionally safe and supported. This might include regular check-ins about each other's feelings, concerns, and joys.
2. Developing Empathy: Work on understanding each other's backgrounds and how they influence current behaviors and feelings. This deeper understanding can help each partner be more empathetic toward the other's reactions and needs.

3. Reinforcing Positive Interactions: Focus on increasing the frequency of positive interactions within the relationship, such as expressing appreciation, spending quality time together, and engaging in mutually enjoyable activities.

Exercises for Building Secure Attachment

Practical exercises can effectively reinforce lessons learned and help integrate secure attachment behaviors into daily relationship dynamics.

- Attachment Mapping: Together, map out what secure attachment looks like for each partner. Discuss scenarios where secure attachment qualities can be applied and plan how to handle situations that typically trigger insecurity.
- Conflict Resolution Role-Play: Engage in role-play exercises to practice handling conflicts in a way that maintains emotional safety and builds trust. These exercises can help partners develop a more constructive approach to disagreements.
- Gratitude Practices: Integrate daily or weekly practices where each partner shares what they appreciate about the other. This not only boosts positive emotions but also strengthens the emotional connection.

Cultivating a path to secure attachment is a transformative journey that requires effort, understanding, and commitment from both partners. By applying these strategies, couples can shift from insecure attachment patterns towards a more stable, secure relationship dynamic. This not only enhances their relationship but also promotes personal growth and well-being for each individual.

As this journey continues, couples build a robust foundation of trust and mutual respect, which not only enriches their relationship but also prepares them to face future challenges together. Through dedicated practice and commitment, the path to secure attachment becomes a rewarding journey that significantly enhances the quality of the relationship and the personal fulfillment of each partner.

Relational Resilience: Preparing for and Prevailing Through Challenges

Relational resilience refers to a couple's ability to effectively navigate and overcome challenges together, emerging stronger and more united. This capacity is crucial for maintaining a healthy, long-lasting relationship, especially when partners come from different attachment backgrounds. This section outlines strategies and practices that help couples build resilience, ensuring they can face life's inevitable stresses and strains without fracturing their bond.

Foundations of Relational Resilience

Building resilience within a relationship involves developing certain foundational qualities and skills that enable partners to withstand and adapt to adversity:

- Mutual Support: Establishing a strong support system within the relationship where each partner feels upheld and valued, particularly during difficult times.
- Flexibility: Cultivating the ability to adapt to changing circumstances and unexpected challenges without losing the core strength of the relationship.
- Positive Communication: Maintaining open lines of communication that emphasize constructive feedback, active listening, and mutual understanding.

Strategies to Enhance Relational Resilience

Implementing specific strategies can significantly bolster a couple's resilience, providing them with the tools they need to manage and overcome challenges together.

1. Stress Management Techniques: Teach each other effective stress management techniques such as mindfulness, meditation, or even physical

activities like yoga or walking. Practicing these techniques together can help mitigate the impact of external stresses on the relationship.

2. Conflict Resolution Training: Engage in conflict resolution training or workshops to learn how to address disputes healthily and productively. Learning to resolve conflicts without damaging the relationship is a key component of resilience.

3. Regular Relationship Audits: Periodically assess the health of the relationship together. Discuss areas of strength and those needing improvement, and make plans for addressing any issues before they become significant problems.

Practical Exercises for Building Relational Resilience

To solidify and practice resilience, couples can engage in exercises designed to strengthen their relationship and prepare them for future challenges:

- Resilience Role-Playing: Role-play potential stressful scenarios to practice how to respond effectively. This exercise helps partners prepare for real-life situations and develop confidence in their ability to handle them.

- Shared Goal Setting: Set goals together that relate to relationship enhancement, such as improving certain aspects of communication or committing to weekly date nights. Working towards common goals can strengthen the partnership and build collective resilience.

- Gratitude and Recognition Exercises: Regularly express gratitude for each other and recognize each other's efforts and achievements. This builds a positive atmosphere that can buoy the relationship during tough times.

Relational resilience is not just about surviving challenges but also about thriving despite them. By fostering mutual support, flexibility, and effective communication, and by regularly practicing resilience-building exercises, couples can enhance their ability to navigate life's challenges together. This not only strengthens the relationship but also enriches the personal development of each partner, making the partnership a source of continuous support and growth.

Through the development of relational resilience, couples ensure that their relationship remains strong, adaptable, and vibrant, regardless of the challenges they face. As partners work together to build this resilience, they lay a robust foundation for a fulfilling and enduring relationship that supports and enhances their lives.

As we conclude this chapter, we prepare to move into the final chapter, which will summarize the key insights from this guide and provide final thoughts on maintaining and nurturing a healthy and resilient relationship.

Chapter 15 Summary

Chapter 15, "Synergizing Attachment Styles," discusses how partners with different attachment styles can work together to create a balanced and harmonious relationship. It emphasizes the importance of understanding and leveraging the complementary qualities of each partner's attachment style. For instance, the stability of a secure partner can help alleviate the anxiety of an anxious partner, and the independence of an avoidant partner can encourage a secure partner to explore their own autonomy.

Key strategies for creating synergy include balancing the needs for closeness and independence, practicing emotional regulation techniques, and enhancing communication. The chapter suggests practical exercises such as role reversal, joint journaling, and creating attachment style "playbooks" to improve understanding and adjust behaviors.

Overall, the chapter advocates for intentional efforts to respect and accommodate each other's attachment needs, promoting a relationship that turns differences into strengths and leads to mutual growth and deeper connection. This approach not only addresses current challenges but also sets a foundation for long-term relationship success, ensuring that partners continue to evolve and enrich their emotional connection.

MY NOTES

Conclusion

This guide has navigated the intricate pathways of relationships, focusing on how understanding, communication, and commitment play pivotal roles in fostering healthy and resilient connections. We've explored a variety of strategies that couples can use to strengthen their bonds and ensure their relationship not only endures but flourishes. As we wrap up, let's reflect on the essential insights offered throughout the guide and consider final thoughts on how to continuously nurture and maintain a thriving relationship.

Key Insights from the Guide

1. *Understanding Attachment Styles*: Recognizing one's own and one's partner's attachment style is fundamental. Each style—be it secure, anxious, avoidant, or fearful-avoidant—carries its unique influence on how individuals engage in relationships. Understanding these styles helps in navigating through emotional complexities, predicting potential issues, and adapting behaviors for a healthier relationship dynamic.

2. *Building Communication Skills*: Effective communication is the cornerstone of any strong relationship. We've seen how active listening, assertive communication, and conflict resolution are not just tools but essential skills that need to be practiced daily to enhance understanding and foster an environment of mutual respect and love.

3. *Enhancing Emotional Intimacy*: Intimacy extends beyond physical interactions; it involves creating a deep emotional connection that is nurtured through transparency, vulnerability, and regular emotional exchanges.

Techniques such as emotional check-ins, shared vulnerability exercises, and intimacy-building activities are critical for deepening this emotional bond.

4. ***Fostering Mutual Support and Flexibility***: Successful relationships are adaptable. They require both partners to support each other not only during easy times but also through significant challenges. Flexibility in handling unexpected changes and stresses, while maintaining a supportive stance, is crucial for long-term resilience and satisfaction.

5. ***Cultivating Resilience***: We've explored how relational resilience can be built through jointly tackling life's adversities, managing stress together, and engaging in positive interactions that reinforce the partnership. This resilience is key to transforming potential relationship pitfalls into strengthening moments.

6. ***Promoting Continuous Growth***: Just as individuals evolve, so too must relationships. Encouraging each other's personal development, continually updating relationship goals, and participating in joint learning activities are ways to keep the relationship dynamic and progressive.

Final Thoughts on Maintaining and Nurturing Relationships

The journey of a relationship is continuous and requires sustained effort from both partners. Here are some enduring strategies to keep your relationship vibrant and healthy:

- ***Commit to Continuous Learning***: Always be open to learning—about each other, about relationships, and about the tools that can help you navigate the complexities of love. This mindset not only helps in adapting to changes but also in overcoming obstacles that come your way.

- ***Prioritize Relationship Health***: Like any important aspect of life, relationships require time and energy. Prioritizing your relationship means actively setting aside time for nurturing it, whether through daily rituals, weekly date nights, or periodic relationship reviews.

- ***Embrace Teamwork***: View your relationship as a partnership in which both members are equally invested. Work together not just in times of crisis but also in planning for the future and making everyday decisions.
- ***Cultivate a Culture of Appreciation***: Regular expressions of gratitude and appreciation can significantly boost the morale and happiness within a relationship. Make it a habit to verbally acknowledge and show appreciation for your partner's actions and qualities.
- ***Seek Joy Together***: Strive to incorporate joy and playfulness into your relationship. Shared moments of happiness build emotional buffers against stress and deepen your connection.

In conclusion, maintaining a thriving relationship is an ongoing process of mutual effort, understanding, and adjustment. By applying the principles and strategies discussed in this guide, couples can ensure that their relationship not only survives but also thrives, enriched by every step of their shared journey. Keep these insights close as you continue to build and enjoy a fulfilling and resilient partnership.

Afterword by a Leading CBT Practitioner

As a seasoned Cognitive-Behavioral Therapy (CBT) practitioner specializing in relationships and attachment issues, I have had the privilege of witnessing the profound impact that CBT can have on individuals struggling with various attachment styles. This afterword aims to provide insights into how CBT can be effectively utilized to address these challenges, enhancing relationship health and personal growth.

The Role of CBT in Understanding Attachment

Attachment issues often stem from early experiences in one's life that shape how individuals perceive and react to closeness and intimacy in relationships. CBT is instrumental in unpacking these deep-seated patterns and provides a structured approach to modifying unhelpful beliefs and behaviors.

- Identifying Cognitive Distortions: CBT helps individuals recognize and challenge the automatic negative thoughts that often underlie insecure attachment behaviors. For example, thoughts like "I am unworthy of love" or "Others will inevitably leave me" can perpetuate avoidant or anxious behaviors.
- Behavioral Experiments: CBT encourages individuals to test the validity of their beliefs through behavioral experiments. For instance, someone who fears rejection might be encouraged to initiate a conversation with their partner about their needs, thereby learning that expressing vulnerability can actually strengthen the relationship rather than weaken it.

Enhancing Emotional Regulation

One of the core components of CBT is teaching individuals to regulate their emotions effectively. This is particularly crucial for those with attachment issues, who may experience intense emotional reactions in close relationships.

- Mindfulness and Emotional Awareness: CBT integrates mindfulness techniques that help individuals become more aware of their emotional states without immediately reacting to them. This awareness creates a space between feeling and action, allowing for more thoughtful and less reactive responses.
- Stress Reduction Techniques: Techniques such as deep breathing, progressive muscle relaxation, and guided imagery are taught to help manage the physiological symptoms of stress and anxiety that often accompany attachment issues.

Improving Communication and Relationship Dynamics

CBT offers practical tools for improving communication skills, which are vital for building and maintaining healthy relationships.

- Assertiveness Training: Many individuals with attachment issues either withdraw or become overly demanding when their attachment anxieties are triggered. CBT helps these individuals learn to communicate their needs and desires assertively and respectfully, ensuring both partners feel heard and valued.
- Conflict Resolution: CBT strategies are used to teach couples how to engage in conflict constructively rather than destructively. This includes learning to identify and articulate one's feelings and needs during disagreements and responding to partner's concerns without defensiveness or retaliation.

The application of CBT to attachment issues is not just about alleviating symptoms but fundamentally transforming the way individuals think about and engage in relationships. Through CBT, individuals learn to build new narratives about their worthiness of love and belonging, which are crucial for developing secure attachments.

For anyone struggling with attachment issues, or for therapists working with such clients, embracing CBT's principles and techniques can lead to meaningful changes—not only in how individuals relate to others but also in how they view themselves.

It is a journey of self-discovery and relationship enhancement that requires patience, commitment, and, most importantly, the courage to change.

MY NOTES

10-Day Challenge to Overcome Fear of Intimacy

Overview of the Challenge

Welcome to the 10-Day Challenge to Overcome Fear of Intimacy. This program is designed to help you confront and move beyond the fears that have held you back from forming deep, meaningful relationships. Whether these fears stem from past experiences, ingrained beliefs, or avoidance patterns, this challenge will guide you through a series of structured exercises and reflections aimed at fostering greater emotional closeness.

What the Challenge Entails

Over the next ten days, you will engage in daily activities that progressively build upon each other to explore and understand your feelings about intimacy. Each day focuses on a specific theme crucial to developing closer personal connections. These themes include understanding your own attachment style, improving self-esteem, effectively communicating needs, managing rejection, embracing vulnerability, building trust, and exploring both emotional and physical intimacy.

The activities range from journaling and self-reflection to practical exercises and discussions with trusted individuals. These are designed to be accessible and manageable, regardless of your current relationship status or past experiences.

What Participants Can Expect to Achieve

By the end of this challenge, you should expect to achieve several key outcomes:

1. **Increased Self-Awareness**: Gain a clearer understanding of the underlying causes of your fear of intimacy, and how your past experiences and attachment style influence your current relationship behaviors.

2. **Improved Communication Skills**: Learn how to express your needs and boundaries more clearly and confidently, which is essential for building healthier relationships.

3. **Enhanced Emotional Resilience**: Develop strategies to handle rejection and setbacks more constructively, reducing the fear associated with opening up to others.

4. **Deeper Emotional Connections**: Through exercises in vulnerability and trust-building, begin to break down the walls that prevent you from achieving intimacy, allowing you to form stronger bonds with others.

5. **A Personalized Roadmap for Growth**: Create a customized plan to continue your journey toward greater intimacy beyond the scope of this challenge, helping to ensure lasting change.

This challenge is not just about overcoming fears; it's about equipping you with the tools and confidence to build the kind of relationships you desire and deserve. Ready to get started? Turn to Day 1 and begin your journey towards a more connected and fulfilling life.

Goals and Objectives: Define clear goals for overcoming fear of intimacy.

As you embark on the 10-Day Challenge to Overcome Fear of Intimacy, it is crucial to set clear, attainable goals. These goals will guide your journey, providing a focused path toward developing deeper connections and overcoming the barriers that intimacy fears can create. Here are the primary objectives of this challenge:

Increase Understanding of Personal Attachment Styles

- **Objective**: Identify your attachment style and understand how it influences your behavior and interactions in relationships. This foundational knowledge will help you pinpoint specific areas where you may need to focus your efforts to become more comfortable with intimacy.

Develop Effective Communication Skills

- **Objective**: Learn and practice effective ways to communicate your needs, desires, and boundaries. This includes enhancing your ability to listen and respond empathetically, as well as expressing yourself openly and honestly without fear.

Build Emotional Resilience

- **Objective**: Strengthen your ability to handle emotional challenges, particularly rejection and criticism, without withdrawing. By improving your resilience, you will be better equipped to face the vulnerabilities that come with close relationships.

Cultivate Trust and Vulnerability

- **Objective**: Engage in exercises that encourage vulnerability and trust-building with others. These activities will help break down barriers to intimacy by fostering a safer emotional environment for sharing and connection.

Enhance Self-Esteem and Self-Acceptance

- **Objective**: Boost your self-esteem and foster greater self-acceptance through reflections and affirmations. Recognizing your worth and learning to appreciate yourself as you are is key to feeling deserving of intimate relationships.

Practice Physical and Emotional Closeness

- **Objective**: Gradually increase your comfort level with both emotional and physical closeness. Through guided activities, learn to relax and enjoy being close to others, which is essential for forming and maintaining intimate relationships.

Create a Personal Growth Plan

- **Objective**: Develop a tailored plan for continuing to advance in your journey toward overcoming fear of intimacy beyond the initial 10-day challenge. This plan should include specific, actionable steps that you can take to maintain and build on the progress you've achieved.

By setting these goals, you will have a roadmap to guide you through the daily activities and reflections of this challenge. Each step is designed to build upon the last, helping you to gradually open up and embrace intimacy without overwhelming fear or anxiety.

How to prepare mentally and emotionally for the next ten days.

Embarking on the 10-Day Challenge to Overcome Fear of Intimacy is a significant step towards personal growth and deeper relational connections. To make the most of this journey, it's essential to prepare both mentally and emotionally. Here's how you can set the stage for a transformative experience:

Reflect on Your Intentions

- **Self-reflection**: Before beginning, spend some time reflecting on why you are taking this challenge. What do you hope to achieve? Understanding your motivations will help you stay committed and open throughout the process.

Create a Supportive Environment

- **Physical space**: Designate a quiet, comfortable space where you can engage in the daily activities without interruptions. Whether it's a corner of your bedroom or a spot at your dining table, ensure it feels safe and calming.

- **Emotional support**: Inform a trusted friend or family member about your commitment to this challenge. Having someone to share your insights and breakthroughs with can provide encouragement and additional perspective.

Schedule Daily Time

- **Consistency is key**: Set aside a specific time each day to work on the challenge's activities. Whether it's in the morning before your day starts or in the evening when you can wind down, having a consistent routine will help you maintain focus and momentum.

Equip Yourself with Necessary Tools

- **Materials**: Ensure you have the necessary tools at hand, such as a journal, pens, and perhaps a meditation app or relaxation music that can aid in your exercises. Having these ready in advance will streamline your daily sessions.

Set Realistic Expectations

- **Be patient with yourself**: Understand that growth often comes gradually and setbacks are part of the process. Recognize that every small step forward is a victory in building intimacy and overcoming fears.

- **Embrace vulnerability**: Prepare to be challenged and to step outside your comfort zone. This challenge will push you to confront uncomfortable truths and habits, but doing so is key to making meaningful changes.

Practice Mindfulness

- **Stress management**: Begin practicing mindfulness techniques such as deep breathing or meditation to help manage stress and anxiety. These skills will be valuable as you navigate the emotional depths of this challenge.

Commit to Honesty

- **Personal honesty**: Commit to being honest with yourself throughout the challenge. True progress can only be made if you are willing to confront and accept your feelings and behaviors candidly.

By preparing yourself in these ways, you'll be better equipped to tackle each day's activities effectively and to handle the emotional ups and downs that may arise. Remember, this challenge is a journey of self-discovery that promises to enhance your ability to connect with others in a meaningful way.

Day 1: Understanding Your Fear

Welcome to the first day of your 10-Day Challenge to Overcome Fear of Intimacy. Today, you will begin by exploring the roots of your fears related to intimacy. Understanding where these fears come from is a crucial step in addressing them effectively.

Activity: Journaling the Roots of Your Intimacy Fears

Objective: Identify and document the underlying causes of your fear of intimacy. This will help you recognize specific experiences, beliefs, or messages that may have contributed to your current feelings about close relationships.

Instructions:

1. **Prepare Your Journal**: Choose a quiet place where you won't be disturbed, and get your journal or a piece of paper ready. If you prefer, you can use a digital document on your computer or tablet.

2. **Reflect on Your Past**: Think about your early relationships, starting with your family and then moving to your early friendships and romantic relationships. Try to recall specific instances where you felt hurt, rejected, misunderstood, or overwhelmed in these relationships.

3. **Identify Patterns**: As you reflect, try to identify any patterns that emerge. For example, were there consistent types of situations, comments, or behaviors that made you feel unsafe or unloved? Write these down.

4. **Consider External Influences**: Think about the messages you received about relationships and intimacy while growing up. These could be from family, culture, media, or religion. How might these messages have shaped your views on intimacy?

5. **Explore Current Beliefs**: Based on these reflections, write down your current beliefs about intimacy and relationships. For instance, do you believe that showing vulnerability will lead to pain? Or perhaps that others can't be trusted not to hurt you?

6. **Acknowledge Your Feelings**: As you journal, it's important to acknowledge any feelings that arise. This process can evoke strong emotions; remember that it's okay to feel whatever comes up. This is part of understanding and Reflection: Identifying patterns and triggers from past relationships.

As you complete Day 1 of your 10-Day Challenge to Overcome Fear of Intimacy, take some time to deeply reflect on what you've uncovered through your journaling activity. Identifying patterns and triggers from your past relationships is a critical step in understanding how these elements continue to influence your current behavior and emotional responses within intimate settings.

Step-by-Step Reflection Process

1. Analyze Common Themes: Review your journal entries and note any recurring themes or situations. Did certain types of events or behaviors consistently lead to discomfort or withdrawal in your past relationships? For example, you might notice that criticism or conflict often led to you distancing yourself from others.

2. Recognize Emotional Responses: Consider the emotional reactions you had in these situations. Did you feel anxious, scared, angry, or perhaps numb? Understanding your emotional responses can help you connect how these feelings play into your current fears of intimacy.

3. Link to Present Fears: Reflect on how these past experiences and the emotions they evoked might be influencing your present-day fears. For instance, if you frequently felt abandoned or criticized, you might now find it hard to believe that you can depend on others or be good enough for them.

4. Consider Behavioral Outcomes: Think about how these emotions and experiences have shaped your behavior in relationships. Do you tend to shut down when someone gets too close, or perhaps preemptively distance yourself to avoid potential pain?

5. Acknowledge Growth Opportunities: Identify which aspects of these patterns you would like to change. Recognizing these areas is not about assigning blame to yourself or others but about acknowledging where there is room for growth and healing.

6. Set Intentions for Change: As you identify these patterns, set clear intentions about how you want to address them moving forward. This might involve practicing more open communication, setting healthier boundaries, or working on self-esteem issues that contribute to your intimacy fears.

Tools for Continued Reflection

- **Keep a Daily Log:** Throughout this challenge, continue to keep a journal of your emotional reactions and thoughts as you engage in the daily activities. This ongoing reflection can help reinforce your discoveries and insights from today.

- **Mindfulness Practices:** Incorporate mindfulness practices such as meditation or mindful breathing into your daily routine. These practices can help you become more aware of your emotional triggers as they occur in real-time, providing you with immediate opportunities to practice different responses.

- **Visual Reminders:** Create visual reminders of the patterns you want to change and your intentions for doing so. These can be notes placed in your living space or reminders set on your phone that encourage you to reflect and stay mindful of your goals throughout the day.

Today's reflection is a foundational step in your journey towards overcoming fears of intimacy. By understanding and acknowledging the roots and triggers of these fears, you set the stage for meaningful change and deeper connections in your relationships.

Day 2: Learning About Attachment Styles

Introduction

On Day 2 of your 10-Day Challenge to Overcome Fear of Intimacy, we delve into understanding different attachment styles. By identifying your attachment style, you gain insight into how you relate to others in intimate relationships. This knowledge is crucial for recognizing patterns that may be barriers to closeness and learning how to adjust them for healthier, more connected relationships.

Activity: Quiz to Determine Your Attachment Style

Objective: Identify your personal attachment style to better understand your behavior patterns in relationships.

Quiz Instructions:

1. **Setup:** Find a quiet space where you can reflect on your past and current relationships without distractions. Have a pen and paper or a digital device ready to record your answers.

2. **Answer Honestly:** As you go through the questions, aim to answer as honestly as possible based on your general tendencies in romantic relationships.

3. **Scoring:** After completing the quiz, use the scoring guide provided to determine your predominant attachment style.

Sample Quiz Questions:

1. When someone I am dating starts getting close, I often find myself pulling away or desiring more space.
   - Always
   - Often
   - Sometimes
   - Rarely
   - Never

2. I worry that romantic partners don't really love me or won't want to stay with me.
   - Always
   - Often
   - Sometimes
   - Rarely
   - Never

3. I find it easy to be emotionally open with partners.
   - Always
   - Often
   - Sometimes
   - Rarely
   - Never

4. I prefer not to share my personal worries or problems with romantic partners.

- Always
- Often
- Sometimes
- Rarely
- Never

5. I often worry about being abandoned.
    - Always
    - Often
    - Sometimes
    - Rarely
    - Never

Scoring Guide:
- **Mostly 'Always' or 'Often' to Questions 1 and 4:** Indicative of an Avoidant Attachment Style.
- **Mostly 'Always' or 'Often' to Questions 2 and 5:** Suggestive of an Anxious Attachment Style.
- **Mostly 'Always' or 'Often' to Question 3:** Reflective of a Secure Attachment Style.

You can supplement and evaluate the result of this test with the self-assessment you did earlier in the book.

Reflection: Connecting Attachment Style to Intimacy

Objective: Reflect on how your attachment style influences your approach to intimacy and relationships.

Reflection Process:
1. **Review Your Results:** Think about how the characteristics of your attachment style may have shaped past relationship dynamics.

2. **Identify Patterns:** Consider how your attachment style influences your reaction to closeness and emotional intimacy. Do you push away, cling, or feel comfortable with closeness?

3. **Link to Personal Experiences:** Recall specific instances in your relationships where your attachment style clearly influenced your behavior. Write these instances down and reflect on the outcomes.

Tools for Further Exploration and Adaptation

- **Read About Attachment Styles:** To deepen your understanding, read books or articles on attachment theory. Excellent resources include *Attached* by Amir Levine and Rachel Heller, and *The Power of Attachment* by Diane Poole Heller.

- **Discuss With a Therapist:** If you find aspects of your attachment style troubling, consider discussing them with a therapist. They can provide personalized strategies to address and possibly reshape your attachment behaviors.

- **Mindfulness Practices:** Engage in mindfulness exercises that help you become more aware of your emotions and reactions as they occur, particularly in the context of relationships.

By understanding your attachment style, you set the stage for meaningful transformations in how you engage with others. Tomorrow, we will focus on building self-esteem and self-acceptance, which are critical for engaging more healthily and openly in relationships.

Day 3: The Role of Self-Esteem in Intimacy

Introduction

Welcome to Day 3 of the 10-Day Challenge to Overcome Fear of Intimacy. Today, we focus on self-esteem and self-acceptance—key elements in cultivating a healthy, intimate relationship with others and yourself. High self-esteem enables you to express your needs and emotions confidently, enhancing your capacity for deeper, more meaningful connections.

Activity: Exercises to Boost Self-Esteem and Self-Acceptance

Objective: Enhance your self-esteem and acceptance to foster a more secure and open approach to intimacy.

Exercise 1: Affirmations for Self-Acceptance

Instructions:

1. **Create a List of Positive Affirmations:** Write down affirmations that resonate with your desires to feel worthy and accepted. Examples include "I am worthy of love and respect," "I accept myself fully," and "My feelings are valid."

2. **Daily Practice:** Every morning, stand in front of a mirror, look yourself in the eyes, and repeat these affirmations aloud with conviction. Continue this practice daily to reinforce positive self-perception.

Exercise 2: Success Inventory

Instructions:

1. **Reflect on Past Successes:** Make a list of your achievements and positive qualities. Include everything from personal successes to professional ones, no matter how small.

2. **Journal About the Impact:** For each item on your list, write a few sentences about how it made you feel and the strengths you demonstrated to achieve it. This exercise helps connect your self-esteem with tangible outcomes.

Exercise 3: Self-Compassion Break

Instructions:

1. **Identify a Moment of Distress:** Think of a recent time when you felt bad about yourself.

2. **Practice Compassion:** Speak to yourself about this moment as you would to a dear friend. Acknowledge the pain, validate the feelings, and offer comforting words of encouragement and support.

Reflection: Connecting Self-Esteem with Your Capacity for Intimacy

Objective: Understand how boosting your self-esteem and self-acceptance directly impacts your ability to form intimate relationships.

Reflection Process:

1. **Review the Exercises:** After completing today's activities, take some time to reflect on how they made you feel. Did affirming your positive qualities change how you perceive yourself?

2. **Connect to Intimacy:** Consider how changes in your self-view could affect your relationships. With greater self-esteem and acceptance, how might you approach intimacy differently? Are there ways you might express your needs or emotions more openly?

3. **Plan Forward:** Based on today's insights, identify specific actions you can take to continually improve your self-esteem in relation to intimacy. This might include setting boundaries, asking for what you need, or expressing your emotions more freely in your relationships.

Tools for Ongoing Practice

- **Maintain a Daily Journal:** Keep a daily journal of your feelings and thoughts about yourself and your interactions with others. Reflect on how your self-esteem affects these interactions.

- **Continue with Affirmations:** Regularly update and practice your affirmations to align with your growing sense of self-worth.

- **Seek Feedback:** Occasionally, ask close friends or loved ones for positive feedback and what they value about you. Use this feedback to reinforce your self-acceptance and understand how others appreciate your qualities.

By focusing on enhancing your self-esteem and self-acceptance, you lay a critical foundation for overcoming fears of intimacy. Tomorrow, we'll build on these concepts by exploring how to effectively communicate your needs and boundaries, further strengthening your ability to engage in healthy, intimate relationships.

Day 4: Communicating Needs and Boundaries

Introduction

Day 4 of the 10-Day Challenge to Overcome Fear of Intimacy is focused on a critical component of building deep and secure relationships: effectively communicating your needs and boundaries. Today, you will engage in role-playing exercises designed to enhance your ability to express your needs clearly and set boundaries respectfully, which are vital for establishing trust and understanding in any relationship.

Activity: Role-Playing Scenarios to Practice Expressing Needs and Boundaries

Objective: Develop the confidence and skills to articulate your needs and establish boundaries in a way that respects both your wellbeing and that of others.

Preparation:

1. **Choose a Quiet Space:** Find a comfortable and private area where you can focus without interruptions.

2. **Select a Partner:** If possible, choose a trusted friend or family member to participate in the role-playing. If you prefer to practice alone, consider using a mirror or recording device to observe and refine your approach.

Scenario Instructions:

1. **Scenario Setup:** Write down or select pre-defined scenarios that commonly occur in relationships where expressing needs or setting boundaries might be necessary. Each scenario should be relevant to your own experiences or fears.

2. **Role-Playing:** Take turns with your partner acting out each scenario. One person acts as yourself, and the other as a friend, family member, or romantic partner. If practicing alone, enact both roles to explore different perspectives.

3. **Feedback:** After each scenario, provide each other with constructive feedback. Focus on tone, clarity, body language, and the effectiveness of the communication. Adjust and repeat the scenarios to improve your responses.

Sample Scenarios:

- **Scenario 1: Declining an Invitation Politely:** You're invited to a large social gathering, but you prefer a quiet evening. Practice how you would decline the invitation respectfully, expressing your need for solitude.

- **Scenario 2: Requesting Support:** You're feeling overwhelmed with work and would like your partner to help more around the house. Role-play how you would communicate this need without sounding accusatory.

- **Scenario 3: Setting Physical Boundaries:** A friend or family member tends to hug you whenever they see you, but you're not comfortable with this level of physical contact. Practice expressing your boundaries clearly and kindly.

- **Scenario 4: Addressing Overstepping:** Your partner regularly checks your phone, which makes you feel uncomfortable. Role-play how you would address the issue and assert your need for privacy.

Reflection: Connecting Communication with Intimacy

Objective: Reflect on how effectively communicating needs and boundaries can enhance intimacy in your relationships.

Reflection Process:

1. **Analyze Your Comfort Levels:** After completing the role-playing exercises, reflect on how comfortable you felt expressing your needs and boundaries. Were there scenarios that felt more challenging than others?

2. **Consider the Impact on Relationships:** Think about how clear communication of your needs and boundaries might change your current or future relationships. How might it prevent misunderstandings and build mutual respect?

3. **Plan Real-Life Application:** Choose one scenario you practiced today and plan a real-life application. Consider the upcoming opportunities to use this skill and prepare yourself to apply it.

Tools for Continuous Practice:

- **Daily Journaling:** Keep a daily journal of instances where you could have communicated your needs or boundaries better. Reflect on what you would do differently next time.

- **Mindfulness Meditation:** Incorporate mindfulness practices that focus on emotional clarity and calmness, which can aid in stressful interactions.

- **Ongoing Feedback:** Continue to seek feedback from trusted individuals about how you express your needs and boundaries. This ongoing input can be crucial for your growth and development.

Conclusion

By enhancing your ability to communicate your needs and boundaries, you are laying the groundwork for relationships that are not only deeper and more intimate but also healthier and more sustainable. Tomorrow, we'll build on these skills by exploring how to manage rejection sensitively and constructively, further strengthening your relationship resilience.

Day 5: Dealing with Rejection

Introduction

Day 5 of the 10-Day Challenge to Overcome Fear of Intimacy addresses one of the most daunting aspects of deepening relationships: dealing with rejection. Today, you'll learn to apply cognitive restructuring techniques to change your emotional and cognitive responses to rejection. This will help you reshape your narrative around rejection, seeing it not as a personal failure but as a part of human interaction that can lead to growth and resilience.

Activity: Cognitive Restructuring Techniques to Handle Rejection

Objective: Learn to reframe your thoughts about rejection, reducing its impact on your self-esteem and fear of intimacy.

Preparation:

1. **Identify Common Rejection Scenarios:** Write down a few situations where you have felt rejected or fear rejection, whether in romantic relationships, friendships, or family interactions.

2. **Create a Comfortable Space:** Find a quiet spot where you can reflect without disturbances.

Techniques and Steps:

1. **Recognize Automatic Thoughts:** For each scenario, identify the immediate thoughts that come to mind following a perceived rejection. These might include thoughts like "I'm not good enough" or "They don't like me because I'm unlovable."

2. **Challenge These Thoughts:** Use cognitive restructuring to challenge these automatic thoughts. Ask yourself:

   - Is there concrete evidence for this thought?

   - Are there alternative explanations for this rejection?

   - What would I tell a friend who had this thought?

3. **Reframe the Thought:** Replace your initial, negative thoughts with more balanced and rational ones. For example, change "I'm not good enough" to "Not everyone will always connect with me, and that's okay."

4. **Role-Play:** Practice this new way of thinking by role-playing with a friend or in front of a mirror. Speak out your rational responses to your common rejection scenarios.

Reflection: Changing Your Narrative Around Rejection

Objective: Reflect on how changing your thoughts about rejection can alter your emotional responses and impact your relationships.

Reflection Process:

1. **Evaluate Emotional Changes:** After practicing the cognitive restructuring techniques, reflect on how your emotional response to rejection scenarios has changed. Do you feel less anxious or fearful?

2. **Consider Relationships:** Think about how this new narrative could influence your interactions. How might dealing with rejection more healthily affect your current and future relationships?

3. **Plan for Future Rejections:** Consider how you can apply these techniques in real-life situations. Planning can make you feel more prepared and less fearful of potential rejection.

Tools for Continuous Practice:

- **Daily Thought Logs:** Keep a daily log of negative thoughts, particularly those related to rejection. Regularly practice reframing these thoughts to build and reinforce the habit.

- **Mindfulness Meditation:** Use mindfulness to stay present and avoid dwelling on past rejections or fearing future ones. Mindfulness can help you recognize when you're spiraling into negative thought patterns.

- **Support Groups:** Engage with online or local support groups where members share and discuss their experiences with rejection. Learning how others handle rejection can provide new strategies and reduce feelings of isolation.

Conclusion

By reframing how you perceive and react to rejection, you can reduce its sting and lessen its barrier to forming close relationships. Tomorrow, we will explore embracing vulnerability, which will further your ability to engage in deep, meaningful connections without overwhelming fear of rejection. This progressive step is crucial for those looking to move from avoidant or anxious attachment styles towards a more secure attachment style, fostering resilience and open-heartedness in relationships.

Day 6: The Power of Vulnerability

Introduction

Day 6 of the 10-Day Challenge to Overcome Fear of Intimacy explores the transformative power of vulnerability. Today, you will actively engage in opening up about a small vulnerability with someone you trust. This exercise aims to demonstrate that showing your true self can strengthen connections and help you experience intimacy in a meaningful way.

Activity: Sharing a Small Vulnerability

Objective: To practice vulnerability in a safe environment and observe how this impacts your feelings and your relationship with the person you choose.

Instructions:

1. **Select a Trusted Person:** Choose someone you feel comfortable with and who has shown understanding and support in the past. This could be a close friend, a family member, or a significant other.

2. **Choose Your Vulnerability:** Pick a vulnerability that is significant but manageable to share. This could be a fear, a personal struggle, a dream you seldom talk about, or an aspect of your self-image that you usually keep hidden.

3. **Set Up a Comfortable Environment:** Arrange to have this conversation in a quiet, private setting where you feel safe. This could be during a walk, over a cup of coffee, or in any space that promotes open dialogue.

4. **Share Your Vulnerability:** Express what you've chosen to share, focusing on being honest and clear. Explain why this is difficult for you and what it means to share it with them.

5. **Discuss Your Feelings:** After sharing, talk about how it felt to open up about this vulnerability. Ask for their thoughts and feelings on what you shared.

Reflection: Reflecting on the Experience and Feelings It Evoked

Objective: To process your emotional responses to sharing a vulnerability and assess how this act of openness impacts your internal narrative about intimacy.

Reflection Steps:

1. **Identify Emotional Reactions:** Note any feelings of discomfort, relief, anxiety, or liberation you experienced during and after sharing.

2. **Evaluate the Response:** Reflect on how the person reacted. Did their response affirm or soothe your fears? How did their reaction affect your feelings of safety and trust?

3. **Consider the Benefits:** Think about the positive outcomes of sharing your vulnerability. Did it lead to a deeper conversation, increased closeness, or a greater understanding between you both?

4. **Acknowledge Your Courage:** Recognize the strength it took to be vulnerable and give yourself credit for taking this step.

Transition to Day 7: Building Trust

As you reflect on today's exercise of vulnerability, consider how these actions lay the groundwork for building deeper trust, which will be the focus of Day 7. Trust is a fundamental component of any close relationship and grows stronger when both parties can openly share and respect each other's vulnerabilities. Tomorrow, you will engage in trust-building exercises that not only test but also strengthen the bonds you share with others, allowing you to cultivate relationships where both vulnerability and trust coexist harmoniously.

Day 7: Building Trust

Introduction

On Day 7 of your 10-Day Challenge to Overcome Fear of Intimacy, we focus on actively building and reinforcing trust with a partner or close friend. Trust is the cornerstone of any deep and lasting relationship. Today's activities are designed to strengthen the trust you share, proving that reliable bonds can transform the quality of your connections and pave the way for more open emotional and physical intimacy in the days to come.

Activity: Trust-Building Exercises

Objective: To engage in exercises that enhance trust through actions and communication, reinforcing the reliability and safety within your relationships.

Instructions:

1. **Choose Your Partner:** Select a partner or close friend whom you wish to deepen your trust with. Ensure this person is someone who has shown an interest in developing your relationship further.

2. **Plan Trust Exercises:**

- **Exercise 1: Blindfold Walk.** One partner is blindfolded and must rely on the verbal guidance of the other to navigate a simple obstacle course (like walking through a park). Switch roles after completing the course.

- **Exercise 2: Two Truths and a Lie.** Each person shares three statements about themselves—two truths and one lie. The other person has to guess which one is the lie, fostering attention and care in listening.

- **Exercise 3: Secret Keeper.** Share something personal that you haven't shared widely, something significant but not overwhelming. Discuss why this is important to keep confidential and let the act of sharing deepen the mutual trust.

3. **Execute with Mindfulness:** As you perform these exercises, focus on the feelings of reliability, safety, and mutual respect. Pay attention to the level of comfort and anxiety, and discuss these feelings openly with your partner.

Reflection: Evaluating Trust Dynamics in Your Closest Relationships

Objective: To assess how trust plays a role in your relationships and how today's exercises might influence these dynamics moving forward.

Reflection Steps:

1. **Analyze Comfort Levels:** Reflect on how comfortable you felt during the trust exercises. Were there moments of hesitation or discomfort? What does this reveal about your current state of trust?

2. **Discuss Outcomes:** Talk with your partner about how the exercises felt for each of you. Discuss any surprises, challenges, or moments of particular importance that arose.

3. **Identify Trust Patterns:** Consider the patterns of trust in your relationship. Are there consistent behaviors that build trust or actions that tend to erode it? How can you address these patterns?

4. **Plan for Continual Trust-Building:** Based on today's experiences, plan how you might continue to build trust. Consider regular activities that reinforce trust, such as weekly check-ins or monthly trust exercises.

Transition to Day 8: Exploring Physical Intimacy

Having strengthened the foundation of trust with your partner, you are now better prepared to explore deeper levels of intimacy. On Day 8, you will engage in activities designed to enhance your comfort with physical closeness. This progressive approach ensures that as you move forward, both emotional and physical expressions of intimacy become more natural and fulfilling, building on the trust and mutual respect established today.

Day 8: Physical Intimacy

Introduction

Building on the trust cultivated on Day 7, Day 8 of your 10-Day Challenge to Overcome Fear of Intimacy invites you to explore physical intimacy. Today's activities focus on experiencing and increasing your comfort with physical closeness in a way that respects your boundaries and those of your partner. This step is vital for fostering a deeper connection and helping you feel more present and engaged in intimate moments.

Activity: Engaging in a Comfortable Level of Physical Closeness

Objective: To gently explore physical intimacy with a partner or close friend, enhancing your comfort level through controlled and consensual touch.

Instructions:

1. **Set Clear Boundaries:** Before beginning, have a conversation with your partner about each other's comfort levels. Discuss and agree on what types of physical interaction you are both comfortable exploring.

2. **Choose Activities:**

   - **Hand Holding Exercise:** Start with something as simple as holding hands while taking a walk. Focus on the sensation of touch, the warmth, and the pressure of the grip.

   - **Hug for Twenty Seconds:** Engage in a twenty-second hug, which is said to increase the hormone oxytocin, known to boost trust and reduce stress.

- **Shoulder Massage:** With permission, give each other a gentle shoulder massage. Concentrate on being present in the moment and responsive to your partner's comfort.

3. **Mindful Engagement:** As you engage in these activities, be fully present. Notice the warmth, the textures, and any emotional reactions that these interactions elicit. If discomfort arises, acknowledge it and discuss it with your partner to adjust accordingly.

Reflection: Observing and Journaling About Your Physical Responses

Objective: To reflect on your physical and emotional responses to increased physical closeness and identify any barriers you may still feel towards physical intimacy.

Reflection Steps:

1. **Journal Your Immediate Reactions:** Right after the activity, take a few moments to journal your initial reactions. How did you feel during the physical interactions? Comfortable, anxious, relaxed, tense?

2. **Analyze Your Comfort Levels:** Reflect on how your comfort levels changed during the activities. Did you become more relaxed over time, or did your discomfort persist? What thoughts were going through your mind?

3. **Identify Emotional and Physical Barriers:** Consider any emotional or physical responses that might serve as barriers to intimacy. Are there specific triggers that make you uncomfortable? How might these be related to your past experiences or fears?

4. **Plan for Progression:** Based on today's reflections, think about small steps you can take to gradually increase your comfort level with physical intimacy.

This could include repeating today's activities regularly or introducing new ones slowly.

Transition to Day 9: Emotional Intimacy

With an enhanced understanding and experience of physical closeness, you are now better prepared to delve deeper into emotional intimacy. Day 9 will focus on using deep conversation prompts to explore emotional landscapes with a partner or friend, building on the trust and physical comfort established to foster deeper emotional connections. This progression ensures a holistic approach to overcoming fears of intimacy, paving the way for profound and enduring relationships.

Day 9: Emotional Intimacy

Introduction

Following the exploration of physical intimacy, Day 9 of the 10-Day Challenge to Overcome Fear of Intimacy shifts focus towards deepening emotional connections. This day is about engaging in meaningful conversations that foster understanding and closeness, allowing you to express and explore emotions with a partner or close friend in a safe and supportive environment.

Activity: Deep Conversation Prompts to Explore with a Partner or Friend

Objective: To facilitate deeper emotional understanding and strengthen the bonds of intimacy through guided conversations.

Instructions:

1. **Prepare the Environment:** Choose a quiet, private space where you both feel safe and free from interruptions. Ensure both of you are in a calm state of mind, perhaps after a brief meditation or a relaxing walk together.

2. **Use Guided Prompts:** Begin with lighter questions and gradually move to more profound topics. Here are some prompts to use:

   - **Lighter Starters:** Begin with easy topics to warm up and establish a comfortable pace for the conversation. Use these questions not just to chat but to start tuning into each other's emotional states and communication styles.

     Examples:

     "What has been the highlight of your day so far?"

     "Are there any small things that have made you smile recently?"

   - **Progressing Deeper:** Transition to topics that require more reflection, tapping into memories and experiences that have impacted your lives. These questions should encourage storytelling and sharing personal insights.

     Examples:

     "What event in your childhood do you think has played an important role in shaping the person you are today?"

     "Can you share a time when you felt truly understood by someone? What did that experience feel like?"

- **Deeply Personal:** Delve into topics that explore core values, fears, and aspirations. These questions are intended to open up deeper levels of vulnerability and foster a profound connection.

  Examples:
  "What is a fear that you've found hard to share with others? How does it influence your daily life?"
  "Imagine describing a fulfilled life. What key elements are part of that picture for you? How does your current path align with that vision?"

3. **Practice Active Listening:** When your partner is speaking, focus fully on listening rather than planning what you'll say next. Show empathy and validation through nods, verbal affirmations, or by paraphrasing their points to show you understand.

4. **Switch Roles:** Ensure both partners have equal time to share and explore their thoughts and feelings. The role of speaker and listener should switch fluidly and frequently to maintain balance.

Reflection: Reflection on the Emotional Connection and Any Barriers Felt

Objective: To reflect on the depth of the emotional connection established through the conversation and identify any barriers that may have emerged.

Reflection Steps:

1. **Immediate Emotional Responses:** After the conversation, take a moment to jot down how you felt. Were there moments of strong emotional resonance or discomfort? Did you discover new feelings about yourself or your partner?

2. **Barriers to Emotional Intimacy:** Reflect on any moments during the conversation where you felt a barrier to intimacy. Was it difficult to answer certain questions, or were there topics you avoided? Consider why these barriers exist and how they might be addressed.

3. **Assessing Emotional Safety:** Evaluate how emotionally safe you felt during this exercise. Did the environment and the interaction foster a sense of security where you could open up, or were there elements of judgment and reservation?

4. **Plans for Enhancement:** Based on your reflections, think about ways to enhance emotional intimacy in your relationships. Are there practices or behaviors you want to develop further? This might involve more frequent deep conversations, establishing new rituals of connection, or seeking external support like therapy if needed.

Guiding Principles for the Conversation:

- **Reciprocity in Sharing:** Ensure both partners have equal opportunities to share and listen. The conversation should flow back and forth, with each person showing genuine interest in the other's responses.

- **Non-judgmental Listening:** Approach the conversation with an open heart and mind. Avoid judging or dismissing feelings and instead, respond with empathy and understanding.

- **Encouragement and Support:** Offer verbal and non-verbal cues to encourage sharing, such as nodding, maintaining eye contact, and using affirmations like "I appreciate you sharing that with me" or "I can see how that would be really challenging."

- **Confidentiality and Trust:** Reinforce the privacy of the conversation, ensuring that all shared information is respected and kept confidential. This fosters trust and reassures both parties that they are in a safe space

Transition to Day 10: Integrating and Moving Forward

Having engaged deeply with both physical and emotional intimacy, Day 10 will focus on integrating these experiences into a cohesive action plan for future growth. You'll reflect on all that you've learned and experienced during this challenge and set practical, achievable goals to continue nurturing and expanding your capacity for intimacy in all forms. This final day will solidify the progress made and prepare you for sustained personal development and deeper relational engagements.

Day 10: Integrating and Moving Forward

Activity: Creating a Personal Action Plan for Continuing Progress in Intimacy

As you reach the final day of this 10-Day Challenge, it's time to consolidate the insights and progress you've made and plan how to integrate and maintain these changes in your daily life.

Objective

Develop a personalized action plan that outlines specific strategies and steps to continue enhancing your capacity for intimacy.

Instructions

1. Review Your Journey:

- Start by revisiting your journal entries and any notes you've made throughout the challenge. Reflect on the key discoveries about your fears, attachment style, self-esteem, communication, vulnerability, and trust.

2. Assess Your Progress:

- Evaluate the changes you've noticed in yourself. How has your understanding of intimacy evolved? In what ways have you grown in your emotional expressions and connections with others?

3. Identify Continuing Goals:

- Based on your reflections, identify specific areas where you wish to continue growing. These might include improving communication, deepening emotional connections, or becoming more comfortable with physical closeness.

4. Set Specific, Measurable Goals:

- For each area of continued growth, set clear and measurable goals. These should be specific (what exactly you want to achieve), measurable (how you will know you've achieved it), attainable (within your ability), relevant (important to your personal growth), and time-bound (with a deadline).

5. Plan Practical Steps:

- Break down each goal into actionable steps. For instance, if your goal is to improve communication, one step might be to practice active listening in all your conversations, perhaps starting with at least one conversation per day.

6. Schedule Regular Reviews:

- Decide how often you will review your progress. Monthly reviews can help you stay on track, make adjustments to your plan, and set new goals as needed.

7. Seek Support:

- Consider how you can use your support network to help you meet your goals. This might involve continuing therapy, joining support groups, or setting up regular check-ins with a trusted friend.

8. Establish Rewards:

- Set up a system to reward yourself for meeting certain milestones. Rewards can be a powerful motivator and can help maintain your enthusiasm for the process.

Reflection: Reflecting on the Growth Over the Challenge and Setting Future Goals

1. Reflect on Achievements:

- Spend some time reflecting on what you have achieved during this challenge. What are you most proud of? What were the most significant changes you noticed in yourself?

2. Identify Challenges:

- Acknowledge any challenges you faced. How did you overcome them? Are there ongoing challenges that need further action?

3. Future Aspirations:

- What are your long-term aspirations regarding intimacy? How do you envision your relationships evolving?

4. Continuous Learning:

- Consider how you can continue learning about intimacy and relationships. This could involve reading books, attending workshops, or continuing therapy.

5. Commit to Ongoing Development:

- Make a commitment to continue working on your intimacy skills. Intimacy is a dynamic aspect of relationships that continuously evolves and deepens.

Conclude your reflection by affirming the commitment to yourself and your personal growth. Recognize that overcoming the fear of intimacy is a journey that doesn't end after 10 days; it's a continuous process that requires dedication, courage, and openness to change. Your action plan is a living document that will grow and change as you do, serving as a roadmap toward a more connected and fulfilling life.

Conclusion: Review of Key Insights

As we conclude the 10-Day Challenge to Overcome Fear of Intimacy, it's important to reflect on the journey you've undertaken, the insights gained, and how these have transformed your approach to relationships and intimacy. This conclusion will help cement the lessons learned and guide future progress.

1. Understanding Attachment Styles:

- You've identified your own attachment style and learned how it shapes your interactions in relationships. This understanding is crucial in recognizing why you react certain ways in intimate settings and provides a foundation for change.

2. Self-Esteem and Intimacy:

- The relationship between self-esteem and intimacy has been explored, highlighting how self-perception influences your ability to open up and trust others. Boosting self-esteem has been a critical step in feeling worthy of close, healthy relationships.

3. Communicating Needs and Boundaries:

- You've practiced expressing your needs and setting boundaries, which are essential for healthy relationships. Effective communication prevents misunderstandings and builds a mutual respect that is conducive to intimacy.

4. Managing Rejection:

- The challenge has equipped you with cognitive strategies to handle rejection more constructively, helping to minimize its impact on your self-esteem and willingness to be vulnerable.

5. Embracing Vulnerability:

- By sharing vulnerabilities, you've tested the waters of deeper emotional expression and likely found that it leads to stronger, more authentic connections.

6. Building Trust:

- Trust-building exercises have shown you practical ways to enhance trust in relationships, whether new or established, highlighting its role as a cornerstone of intimacy.

7. Exploring Physical and Emotional Intimacy:

- Activities focused on both physical and emotional intimacy have helped you identify your comfort levels and expand them, thereby deepening connections in a balanced way.

8. Continuous Integration and Growth:

- Finally, creating a personal action plan has set the stage for sustained effort towards enhancing intimacy, ensuring the longevity of your progress.

Changes in Perception of Intimacy

1. Redefining Intimacy:

- Your understanding of what intimacy means has likely expanded beyond physical closeness to include emotional bonding, communication, and shared vulnerability.

2. Overcoming Fear:

- The fear of intimacy, once perhaps a daunting barrier, has been addressed through practical exercises and reflections that demonstrate its manageability and the growth it can foster.

3. Valuing Emotional Connections:

- You may now see emotional connections as integral to your well-being and essential for fulfilling relationships, rather than something to be wary of.

4. Appreciating Personal Growth:

- Throughout this challenge, the focus on personal development has likely shown you that improving your relationship with intimacy also enhances your self-understanding and overall happiness.

Moving Forward

As you move beyond this challenge, keep in mind that overcoming the fear of intimacy is a journey, not a destination. Continue to utilize the tools and insights gained, and allow yourself to grow at your own pace. Regular reflection and adaptation of your action plan will help you stay aligned with your goals and respond to new challenges as they arise. Keep your support systems engaged, and remember that seeking professional help is a strength, not a weakness, whenever you feel stuck.

This challenge is just the beginning of a deeper exploration into forming and sustaining intimate relationships. As you progress, you will likely find that each step forward enriches not only your relationships but also your personal growth and happiness.

Continuing Your Journey: Tips and Strategies for Maintaining and Building on Progress

As you conclude the 10-Day Challenge to Overcome Fear of Intimacy, the journey towards deeper, more fulfilling relationships doesn't end here. Maintaining and building on the progress you've made requires continuous effort and dedication. Here are some effective tips and strategies to help you keep growing and strengthening your intimacy skills:

1. Establish a Routine of Reflection and Practice

- **Daily Reflections:** Set aside a few minutes each day to reflect on your interactions and feelings. This can help you stay aware of your behaviors and the progress you're making in overcoming fears of intimacy.

- **Regular Practice:** Continuously practice the skills you've developed, such as communicating openly, expressing needs and boundaries, and embracing vulnerability. Regular practice helps solidify these skills and make them a natural part of your interactions.

2. Keep Learning and Expanding Your Knowledge

- **Educational Resources:** Continue to educate yourself on topics related to attachment, communication, and emotional well-being. Books, podcasts, and workshops can provide new insights and reinforce your existing knowledge.

- **Professional Guidance:** Consider ongoing therapy or counseling, especially if you find certain aspects of intimacy particularly challenging. A professional can offer personalized support and strategies tailored to your specific needs.

3. Utilize Support Networks

- **Support Groups:** Join online forums or local support groups where you can share experiences and learn from others facing similar challenges. These communities can offer encouragement and different perspectives on handling intimacy issues.

- **Trusted Friends and Family:** Keep communication open with trusted loved ones. Their support can be invaluable as you navigate the complexities of building closer relationships.

4. Expand Your Comfort Zone Gradually

- **New Experiences:** Challenge yourself to step outside your comfort zone by engaging in new activities or social settings. This can help improve your confidence and reduce anxiety associated with new interactions.

- **Incremental Exposure:** Gradually increase the level of emotional or physical closeness in your relationships at a pace that feels manageable. This helps prevent overwhelm and builds resilience over time.

5. Celebrate Achievements and Learn from Setbacks

- **Acknowledge Progress:** Regularly acknowledge and celebrate your achievements, no matter how small. Recognizing your own progress can be a significant motivator.

- **Constructive Handling of Setbacks:** View setbacks as opportunities to learn and grow. Analyze what didn't work and why, and adjust your approach accordingly. This resilience will strengthen your capability to deal with future challenges.

6. Maintain Emotional Health

- **Mindfulness and Meditation:** Continue practices like mindfulness or meditation to maintain emotional balance. These practices can help you stay centered and better manage stress and anxiety.

- **Physical Health:** Never underestimate the impact of physical health on emotional well-being. Regular exercise, a balanced diet, and sufficient sleep are crucial for maintaining the energy and mental clarity needed for building intimacy.

7. Set Future Goals

- **Short-Term and Long-Term Goals:** Define clear, achievable goals for both the short term and the long term. These should focus on areas of intimacy where you feel more growth is needed or possible.

- **Regular Reviews:** Periodically review and adjust your goals to reflect your current situation and aspirations. This ensures that your objectives remain relevant and aligned with your personal growth journey.

8. Create a Personal Journal

- **Ongoing Journaling:** Maintain a journal dedicated to your journey toward overcoming fear of intimacy. Regular entries can help you track patterns, process emotions, and document insights and breakthroughs.

By implementing these strategies, you can continue to build on the foundations laid during the 10-day challenge. Remember, each step forward, no matter how small, is a part of your journey toward richer, more connected relationships.

About the Author

Esther Collins is a renowned psychologist and author, specializing in relationship dynamics and cognitive-behavioral therapy (CBT). With over two decades of experience in clinical practice, Esther has dedicated her career to helping individuals and couples overcome challenges in their personal and relational lives through the application of CBT principles.

Her early fascination with human behavior and emotional wellness propelled her into a career that focuses on the intersections of cognitive processes and interpersonal relationships.

Esther's professional journey includes working in private practice, hospitals, and academic settings, where she has not only treated clients but also mentored emerging psychologists. She is a sought-after speaker at psychology conferences and workshops, where she shares her insights on improving relationship health and emotional functioning using evidence-based strategies.

As an author, Esther has published several influential books, including the well-regarded *Couples Therapy Workbook*, which offers practical exercises and insights for couples looking to deepen their relationships through structured interventions. Her work is characterized by a deep empathy for human struggles and a commitment to providing strategies that are both scientifically sound and practically feasible.

In addition to her clinical practice and writing, Esther serves as a consultant for various mental health organizations, helping to design programs that enhance emotional resilience and relationship stability. She has received numerous awards for her contributions to clinical psychology.

Esther lives in San Francisco with her partner and two children. In her free time, she enjoys hiking, reading, and practicing mindfulness meditation—activities that she often recommends in her therapeutic practice for maintaining personal well-being and a balanced life.

Your Insight Can Illuminate the Path for Others

If you've reached this point in the book, you've journeyed deeply into the complex realms of attachment, intimacy, and personal growth, particularly addressing the challenges of avoidant attachment. You've tackled unveiling independence, vulnerability, and perhaps started reshaping your understanding of intimacy and trust. Now, you're invited to share your unique experiences and insights by leaving an honest review on Amazon. Your feedback not only reflects your own journey but also serves as a guiding light for others navigating similar paths in their relationships.

Imagine the Impact of Your Words

Think of how a single insight from this book changed your perspective or offered a moment of clarity. Your review could be the catalyst for similar epiphanies in others. It could encourage someone to start their journey towards emotional equilibrium, to embrace the discomfort of growth, or to seek understanding in the roots of their relational patterns.

Engage in a Greater Dialogue

Your review helps to weave a tapestry of collective insight that can support, guide, and inspire an entire community of readers. Each shared experience, each story of struggle and triumph, enriches this ongoing dialogue. It's not just about reviewing a book; it's about adding your voice to a chorus of narratives that can uplift and empower.

Thank You for Making a Difference

Your thoughts and experiences are a gift to this community. Together, we can support one another in transforming the way we relate to ourselves and those around us. Please take a moment to leave your honest review on Amazon, and let's continue to build a world where every voice is heard and every heart is understood.

Thank you for your courage to share, your willingness to help others, and your commitment to your journey of growth and healing.

Your voice matters.

Click here or scan this QR code to leave your review on Amazon if you live in the US

https://www.amazon.com/review/create-review/?asin=B0D3B6PH7Y

Click here or scan this QR code to leave your review on Amazon if you live in the UK

https://www.amazon.co.uk/review/create-review/?asin=B0D3B6PH7Y

Click here or scan this **QR** code to leave your review on Amazon if you live in the Canada

https://www.amazon.ca/review/create-review/?asin=B0D3B6PH7Y

Click here or scan this **QR** code to leave your review on Amazon if you live in the Australia

https://www.amazon.com.au/review/create-review/?asin=B0D3B6PH7Y

<u>GET YOUR EXCLUSIVE BONUS HERE!</u>

SCAN THIS QR CODE:

OR

COPY AND PASTE THIS URL:

https://drive.google.com/drive/folders/1JtugbSJsd-dIneVKaaRmU5lEHf4yu2V-?usp=sharing

Made in the USA
Middletown, DE
12 August 2024

58987242R00144